RAISED
BY
UNICORNS

RAISED BY UNICORNS

STORIES FROM PEOPLE WITH LGBTQ+ PARENTS

EDITED BY FRANK LOWE

CLEiS
PRESS

Published in the United States by Cleis Press, an imprint of Start Midnight, LLC, 101 Hudson Street, Thirty-Seventh Floor, Suite 3705, Jersey City, NJ 07302.

Printed in the United States.
Cover design: Scott Idleman/Blink
Text design: Frank Wiedemann
Author photo: Matthew J. Wagner, Fine Photography
First Edition.
10 9 8 7 6 5 4 3 2 1

Trade paper ISBN: 978-1-62778- 256-2
E-book ISBN: 978-1-62778-257-9

Library of Congress Cataloging-in-Publication Data is available on file.

TIME article excerpts from "I Was Ashamed and Silent About Being Raised by Two Women" provided by, and used with the permission of, Time Inc.

TIME article excerpts from "Why Children of Same-Sex Parents Should No Longer Feel Invisible" provided by, and used with the permission of, Time Inc.

CONTENTS

*I dedicate this book to the pioneering LGBTQ+
parents that inspired me to follow in their footsteps,
and to their children that continually inspire
and amaze me.*

EDITOR'S NOTE

H<small>I</small>, I'<small>M</small> F<small>RANK</small> L<small>OWE</small>, a forty-one-year-old divorced gay dad. Some of you may know me from my snarky, acerbic Twitter persona "@GayAtHomeDad." Others may be familiar with my writing for publications such as Huff Post, Gays with Kids, and *The Advocate* online, among many more. When I started tweeting in 2012, my original intent was to blow the roof off gay parenting stigmas. I used humor to diffuse what was a newer concept then (times have changed in five years), and it worked. I amassed over a hundred thousand followers who can now say they know at least *one* gay dad.

I used that platform to segue into what I really wanted to do—help others in the LGBTQ+ community, specifically youth. Through my writing, I opened my life wide open and gave people a true perspective into what it means to be a gay parent. Most readers have discovered there's not really a big difference. Sure, I might put a little more flair into styling my kid's hair, but that's about it. Needless to say, my son is my life, and I've dedicated myself to him becoming the best human possible.

Growing up as a gay kid in the 1970s and 1980s, I never viewed fatherhood as a possibility. Everywhere I looked, images of the LGBTQ+ community were hyperbolic and superficial. I didn't have an idol to admire because "gay" was considered a defect. Much to my surprise, there *were* pioneers and always have been; brave LGBTQ+ individuals who ignored the criticism and became parents when no one dared. To them I will always raise my glass, and extend an appreciation that goes beyond words. But I can assure you, the fight is still raging. There is much work to be done, and many eyes that need opening.

Six million and counting. A huge number, right? Hard to believe when you consider we're discussing U.S. citizens who have at least one LGBTQ+ parent. But that's reality. These people can't even type "my moms" or "my dads" into Microsoft Word without it wanting to add an unnecessary possessive apostrophe—i.e. "my mom's" (try it, you'll be amazed). Whether they want to be or not, they *are* an extension of the LGBTQ+ community. Terms such as *"queerspawn"* have been used to describe them, but personally I wouldn't refer to my son as that. In fact, I don't think he needs a label. He can be what he wants to be.

When people discover that I have a son, the first question is always "how?" I understand the curiosity and happily volunteer the truth. "My now ex-husband and I adopted him from birth, locally." That sums it up very succinctly, and allows me to elaborate, should I choose to. The long version is that we got on the adoption list, were chosen by our birthmother six weeks later, and she had our son nine days after that. It was a whirlwind of happiness and new responsibilities. My joke has always been that straight couples get nine months; we only had nine days.

Prior to our son's birth, I longed for any kind of information about gay adoption and raising a baby. It was 2009, and there were a few popular options. Every night, I'd be awake until three A.M. reading, to absorb all I could. Eventually I wanted something I was unable to find: the viewpoint from kids with LGBTQ+ parents. Now, that isn't to say there weren't choices available (there were and are). I just couldn't locate them easily, and time was not on my side.

Before we knew it, our son Briggs arrived and my priorities shifted immediately. I was fortunate enough to be a stay-at-home dad (hence the infamous Twitter moniker), and my entire life revolved around him. I thought less and less about, "What will he think about all this eventually?" and focused more on "How can I currently improve his life?" Not to say I wasn't empathetic to him, things just changed once he came along.

Fast forward to now—2018—he's eight, and I've never been more proud of a human being in my life. He's been an inspiration to me in infinite ways, including what you're reading right now. I was gifted with this fantastic opportunity, and can finally give voices to those who have been relatively silent or swept under the rug.

"*Raised by Unicorns*" is obviously a take on the old adage "raised by wolves," and I couldn't find it a more fitting title. Not that I necessarily consider myself a unicorn (well, okay, sometimes), but the LGBTQ+ community comprises unique individuals and therefore, it seemed entirely appropriate. My goal was to present a diverse anthology to you, full of different life experiences. These stories run the gamut, and that is the beauty of it all. You may notice that this book is a little heavier on the L and G, but I feel that is a snapshot of the time we are living in and is constantly evolving. I envision this as a first volume, and want to revisit it every decade or so to document the inevitable changes and progress.

All I hope you take away from this book is empathy. These people are beautiful souls who have faced adversity since they were born. Some of the stories might be what you imagine, and others will floor you. Regardless, in a century or so, this will be history, and I thank you for being part of it just by taking all of this in.

To START US off, here is a note from my son, as he is too young to write a chapter:

Hi, my name is Briggs. I'm eight-and-a-half-years-old and in the third grade. I have two dads and they are very nice to me. My dads help me with things. I like that I have two dads. They don't live together anymore, but that's okay—I still see them the same. I get *two* Christmases now. I call one dad "Daddy," and the other one is "O'Daddy." I talk to them every night. I love playing video games with Daddy and playing catch with O'Daddy. I love my dads very, very much!

THE CURIOUS CASE OF A STRAIGHT BOY COMING OUT

ARIEL CHESLER, age 39

As a father to two young daughters who are influenced by Disney movies and other common culture, the topics of love and marriage come up often. But when my daughters discuss marriage with me, they sometimes forget our previous conversations on the topic.

"Isabella says only a boy can marry a girl," one of them reports to me one night at dinner.

"That's not right," I respond. "Two of your grandmothers are married to each other! "That was your first wedding," I tell my older daughter.

"Oh, right," is the response, and we quickly move to the next topic. So simple. No big deal. A shrug. A whatever. No, in truth—a revolution.

Sometimes when things move fast it is too easy to forget what came before. Today, when people talk about marriage equality or children being raised by same-sex couples, it seems they can't even imagine or comprehend how it was. Presently, there are many LGBTQ+ couples who are married and raising children. At any one time, there are almost 100,000 LGBTQ+ couples raising children. Just one type of the many diverse families we have in our country. But the reality of children being raised from birth or infancy in two-parent LGBTQ+ homes is a relatively recent phenomenon.

Television shows like *Modern Family*, and *This Is Us*, children's books like *Heather Has Two Mommies*, or *The Family Book*, have contributed to normalizing these families, these relationships. In so many ways, the kids of same-sex couples today are so much more all right than I was because they can see themselves in books and on screen, which both validates and changes how they view themselves. They also see their families protected equally by our laws. In many different facets, we have reached a point of what appears to be acceptance, equality, maybe even love.

But please know, Dear Reader, that before acceptance there was hate and stigma. And before that, attaining equality, legal rights, or recognition was not even a dream. Instead, there was invisibility and shame. Perhaps people forget because the ecstasy of recent justice blinds them, or perhaps it is a naive belief that because the nation's highest court has recognized same-sex marriage as valid and equal that the war is won, and all that is the past is behind us. But for those of us who were among the first to be raised by LGBTQ+ parents, we cannot forget because we carry scars in the innermost places of our hearts. So please, then, friend, let me share my story of being raised by two women in the 1980s. Let us remember it like it was.

THE FIRST THING you must know about is my shame about being raised by two mothers. Why? Because shame is what has stalled my writing these very words you are reading. Shame has made me pause and pull away and doubt and block my thoughts. Shame is what still makes it more comfortable to keep this story locked away, private, unshared. Shame is what silenced part of my childhood. And, once learned, shame stays with you for a very long time. This is the point of Pride events and Pride marches, isn't it? Showing pride in ourselves and in our families is the opposite of and the antidote to shame, just as visibility is necessary to combat invisibility. Speaking our truth and sharing our stories and doing so with pride is the path to freedom. But, this was not something I could do as a child.

The second thing you must know is that before my shame about having two mothers, I had a deep and ever-present longing for my father. That longing is also still with me and I'm always looking for him. Sometimes, I think I see my father as I walk down crowded New York City streets. I see a man and I am sure that's my father's hair or his stride. It's *never* him. I keep walking.

I was born in Manhattan in January 1978. By all accounts, my father was greatly involved in raising me during my first couple years of life. He fed and changed me, bathed me, and woke in the middle of the night to tend to my needs. Some of my earliest memories are images of my father and Central Park. I see branches and leaves, feel his hand grasping mine, and hear his accented voice speaking to me in Hebrew.

My mother and father divorced when I was two, and I continued to live with my mother in Brooklyn and see my father on alternate weekends. My mother—a trail-blazing feminist author, psychologist, and professor—

was often unavailable to me, and by necessity left me in the hands of nannies and babysitters, and my grandmother. My father's absence from my home and my mother's inability to be more present resulted in my constant thirst for a hands-on parent.

Each time I was to see my father, I sat for countless hours looking out the window of my Brooklyn home, waiting and hoping for him to arrive. He was always late, so I watched the pavement and the passersby, jumping at each car that slowed near my house, thinking it could be my father. Weekends with him were always fun, but they inevitably ended. It was never enough. I needed him for the daily grind, to fulfill the challenging, never-ending role of a parent.

I also longed for a closer connection to my father's family, my extended family in Israel, including my grandparents, aunts, and cousins. My mother had a strained relationship with her brothers and little other family, and so my connection to her blood relatives was inconsistent and insufficient.

Because my dad was not involved in my life in as deep a way as I desired, I always fantasized about his returning to live with me. Often, I couldn't understand why his return was not possible, and I longed for my parents to love each other and be with each other again in the way I'd seen in the black and white photographs taken at the time of my birth.

My father's absence formed an unfillable hole, an insatiable hunger. I was in so much pain and angry at my dad for not being there in the ways I wanted. I didn't need any dad. I needed my dad. And nothing could replace him.

Still, while being a child of divorce was painful, it

was not uncommon and it was not something I had to hide. Other children had absent, distant fathers. Other children only saw their fathers on weekends. Some children I knew had step-dads. Divorce was represented in the popular culture of the time. Just think of the acclaimed 1979 film *Kramer vs. Kramer*, which portrays a divorce's impact on a young boy. I also recall reading *Megan's Book of Divorce*, a children's book by Erica Jong, which normalized my status as a child of divorce, and helped me work through the pain and frustration of not having my father in my home.

As a child with a father absent from my home and an incredibly busy single mother, the last thing I wanted was to share my mother with someone else. It was hard enough for me to accept all the time my mother spent in her home office writing, and all the meetings and events she had to attend.

I had a habit of crawling into my mother's bed in the early morning hours. That was my space, my sacred time with her. One day, when I was five years old, I made my way to her bedside and was shocked to see a second figure in the bed. It was a woman, the woman who became my mother's first long-term girlfriend and my second mother. But, in that moment, for me she was an interloper, an obstacle, an unwanted presence. But she didn't go away. To the contrary, she joined our household.

For a time, I was cold and distant. I wanted nothing to do with that woman. She certainly wasn't my father and I had not agreed to have her live in our home. I became nasty and mean and started name-calling. Unlike my mother, she swiftly disciplined me, and laid down ground rules about my behavior. I listened.

Her name was Patricia. And as she became a permanent fixture in our home, and as we grew to know each other, my position changed. Pat was there every day, after all. She was there in the mornings to make me eggs and English muffins. She was there after school to bring me to activities. She was there in the evenings. She took me to see her parents and to play with her siblings' children on weekends, children I came to consider my cousins. In fact, she was there during all those moments I had been looking for a second parent.

We had meals as a family, and went on vacations to Disney World. Pat taught me how to dance to Michael Jackson and she and my mother encouraged me in all my interests. Pat comforted me when I needed it and disciplined me when I needed it. She empathized with my longing for my father. I saw her express love for my mother, and we became a family. Eventually, I called Pat my "other mother."

Also, Pat gave me, a Jewish-American boy, the greatest gift of all: Christmas. I grew up celebrating Hanukkah, singing all the requisite songs, and lighting the menorah all eight nights. But, Christmas trees and presents excited me. So you could imagine my delight when Pat, who is Italian-American, brought those things into our home. "It was a dream come true, the tree towering over everything save the forest of bookshelves that were its backdrop, bearing ornaments and lights and presents, all forbidden fruit that I was allowed to touch and smell and open. The tree was about custom, not religion. It was about warmth in the winter and complementing our Hanukkah nights, and mostly about making a young boy happy."[1]

During Christmastime, I would slide down the bannister of our Brooklyn brownstone, and rush for a pile of presents beneath the tree. It was with pure glee that I broke into boxes containing He-Man, G.I. Joe figures, and Nintendo games. I would then proudly take Polaroids of myself in the aftermath, beaming, surrounded by my treasure. We would enjoy Italian Christmas feasts with Pat's family. Tables were filled with calamari, fried shrimp, and the pasta dishes I will crave forever.

But the love we shared and the family we created were not known by the world outside our home, by the world of my peers. "I did not talk about it with my closest friends, with whom I shared everything from my fears and anger to my crushes on girls. Even though some of these friends were in my home on a weekly basis, it was simply not discussed. Not by me. Not by them. Never."[2] And the reason my family was not discussed was that we had no proper titles, no definitions, no sufficient words to describe who we were to each other. The entire idea of my family was not even imaginable. It was off the radar screen. And heterosexism led most to assume my mother was straight. Case in point: My grandmother thought it was cruel that Pat shared a bedroom with my mother. "If you really cared about her, you'd get her a room of her own," she would chide.

This was the invisibility that led to silence. Silence was easier. But silence is deadly.

There was one exception. I was six or seven years old. A kid at the playground confronted me. He was filled with cockiness because he knew my deep, dark secret.

"I know something about your mom," he began.

"What is it?" I asked.

"Your mom is a lesbian," he spit out.

"So what? I know that," I shot back. "What do you really know about her?" Oh, if only I could have bottled that level of comfort, boldness, and confidence I displayed in that encounter. Was it an act? In any case, I lost that ability because somewhere along the way I learned shame, as every child does.

Perhaps it would have helped me to connect to other families that were like mine. In more recent years, I have been told by other grown children of same-sex couples that they attended Family Week and Pride marches and other events where they could bond with other children of LGBTQ+ parents. Today, we have organizations like COLAGE, "which unites people with lesbian, gay, bisexual, transgender, and/or queer parents into a network of peers, supports them, and allows them to share experiences and create community. This is such important work because allowing us to see other children with common but also unique family stories strengthens us and allows us to be seen as well."[3]

But, my mother never narrowly defined herself by her sexuality. The focus of her work and her social circles was on other issues: women's mental health, reproductive rights, civil rights, sexual and domestic violence, equal pay, custody, and women's religious rights. So, the events I attended and the causes I learned to champion and to give voice to as a child did not include LGBTQ+ issues. On those issues, I was voiceless.

The weight of being voiceless was so great that I broke my silence and "came out" about my family in the oddest way. During my senior year of high school one of my closest friends was a girl. I fell in love with her and we dated briefly. One weekend, she invited me to her family's country house. While there, she decided to end our romantic relationship. This was particularly cruel because I was trapped there, and was made to feel alone. I was so heartbroken that during a break up conversation with my then ex-girlfriend I suddenly began talking about my family. I think I blurted out "my mom is gay," apropos of I have no idea what. "Somehow, the pain of the breakup and the shame I had been holding inside for years became one, and they flowed out of me together."[2] She told me that she already knew what I revealed, but she had never brought it up.

Then, a year later, I participated in a story-sharing panel as part of a college women's studies course. Other participants included a black man who wanted to be respected for his mind, a woman who had suffered domestic violence, a woman who had grown up in poverty, and a gay man who had to come out of the closet. When it was my turn to share, I found it more difficult to tell my story than I thought it would be, and I learned that stories kept hidden for so long are harder to reveal. Ultimately, it was truly liberating to be able to speak about this part of my life after years of avoidance and silence.

It was only after my experiences in college that I was able to return home and share the truth with my childhood friends. Some were shocked. Some had already suspected. All were accepting and supportive. This support was nice but could not undo all the years of silence. So, while it felt good to share my story, it was not an instant fix. On the contrary, because my story was wrapped in pain and shame, it took years of practice speaking it aloud before I could sit more comfortably with it.

SOMETHING ELSE HAPPENED that deeply impacted my childhood. When I was thirteen, my mother and Pat separated. Suffering this cleavage was different but as painful as the split between my mother and father. I was older and more self-sufficient. My mother and Pat had given me the love, discipline, and stability I needed in my formative years. But, I was of course devastated that Pat was leaving, and I knew that she too could never be replaced by anyone else.

I maintained a relationship with Pat much in the same way I did with my father. We spoke on the phone. I looked forward to seeing her on weekend visits and holidays, especially Christmas, which I always celebrated with Pat and her family.

A year after her split with Pat, my mother began a relationship with Susan, her long-time partner (now wife) who is the grandmother to my children. Accepting Susan living in my home was a unique challenge, and for a long time we kept to our own corners. Over time, Susan became family, a mentor and a friend. Yet, I've never had a title for her. Nor she for me. In fact, I often refer to her as my mom's wife. Even my children simply call her "Susan."

Interestingly, all throughout my high school years, while Susan was living with us, none of my friends ever discussed or asked about her relationship to my mom. This is despite the fact that she joined us for family dinners and birthdays, and was always there when my friends hung out or slept over at my house. Once again, their silence allowed for the continuation of my silence. Their inability to imagine that my mother was with a woman permitted me not to address it. And, perhaps, the stigma we all felt deep down mandated that whatever the relationship between my mother and Susan, something was wrong because something was different. Thus, it was safer to keep it invisible and unacknowledged.

I have been with my wife since college. For a long time, I had no interest in and was opposed to getting married, in part because there was not yet marriage equality in New York. I also believed that we didn't need the state to validate our relationship. I already knew its value and our commitment to each other. Because we were both young and employed and had no children, our decision to remain unmarried to each other was largely inconsequential. We were able to live together and share financial burdens, and we were recognized by others as a couple.

And then a funny thing happened on the way to being radical: I lost my job and needed health insurance. Still, hoping to stay true to my principles, we decided to register as domestic partners, despite the fact that the option to marry was available to us as a straight couple. Unfortunately, my wife's employer at the time would only extend health insurance benefits to either same-sex domestic partners or straight married couples. There-fore, faced with no other choice, we returned to City Hall and obtained a marriage license.

Two years after obtaining a marriage license, we had a large and wonderful wedding (which taught me the unique joy of making family and friends happy in publicly recognizing our love and our Jewish traditions). Nevertheless, we insisted on calling our ceremony a ninth-anniversary celebration, because we refused to erase the totality of our relationship. To this day, we do not measure our relationship from the time we were married but from the time we began dating.

A few years later, my mother and Susan had a simple yet meaningful wedding in Connecticut, which had passed marriage equality before New York did. My oldest daughter was only four months old at the time. We made our way to a small pier where we watched sailboats blowing by until a locally ordained official arrived and presided over the brief ceremony. We rounded out the evening with a dinner, just the five of us.

ON MARCH 27, 2013, the United States Supreme Court heard arguments in United States v. Windsor, the case dealing with the constitutionality of the Defense of Marriage Act and the companion case of Hollingsworth v. Perry, the case involving California's Prop 8. I followed the cases with great interest and observed others wearing red or changing their Facebook icons to support marriage equality. But I did not speak out. And then I read the transcript of the oral arguments.

A line from Justice Scalia launched itself out. It was a gut-punch. One I never expected. Noting that some states do not permit same-sex adoption, Scalia asked about the "consequences of raising a child in a . . . single-sex family" and questioned whether "it is harmful to the child or not."

And then Justice Kennedy spoke directly to me.

Noting that many children already live with same-sex parents, Kennedy remarked: "[those children] want their parents to have full recognition and full status. The voice of those children is important in this case, don't you think?"

Something stirred in me and I knew I was obligated to add my voice on this issue. I hastily tapped out a Facebook rant, opening my childhood to the world. The rant soon turned into a piece on Huffington Post[4.] In it, I testified that the notion that two people of the same-sex raising a child might cause the child harm is preposterous and that all that matters to a child is love and support, respect, stability and maybe a little independence, all of which I received. I closed by praying that the Supreme Court does justice, and that all families are recognized as equal throughout this great country.

More pieces followed. In March 2015, before the oral arguments in Obergfell v. Hodges, in which the Supreme Court held that the Fourteenth Amendment requires all states to grant same-sex marriages, I wrote another piece[5]. Responding to Justice Kennedy as one of the children he thought was important to hear from, I told him: "Do it for us." I stressed that "children should not be stigmatized because their families are different from the 'norm,' whether they are raised in an interracial family, in a single-parent household, or by a same-sex couple."[2] And I noted that "when the law does not recognize your family, stigma and fear are perpetuated and reinforced."[2] I declared that it was time for the highest court in our land to reflect a new moral judgment that same-sex couples should no longer be stigmatized, that their relationships should be recognized by the law, and that their children will be better off for it.

In this brave new world of marriage equality, I have tried to share my story as often and as widely as I can in writing and in person. Even with all the progress we have made, the world still doesn't know nearly enough about the estimated six million children in America with an LGBTQ+ parent, and, speaking as one of those children, we don't necessarily know enough about each other. How wonderful would it be if we could access each other's stories? How wonderful would it be if we could be seen and see each other? Some work colleagues and others I encounter are still surprised to hear my tale. I've even had to educate my own daughters about it. I'm counting on them to teach their classmates about love, inclusion, and how their dad grew up. My greatest hope is that in the future when my daughters tell their story of having three grandmas, their peers will turn to them and say, "I've heard that one before."

---

1   Ariel Chesler, "My Ghost of Christmas Past," Tablet Magazine, Nextbook Inc., December 16, 2014, 13:36, http://www.tabletmag.com/scroll/187712/my-ghost-of-christmas-past

2   Ariel Chesler, "I Was Ashamed and Silent About Being Raised by Two Women," Time, Time Inc., March 6, 2015, http://time.com/3735410/same-sex-marriage-children-gay-parents/

3   Ariel Chesler, "Why Children of Same-Sex Parents Should No Longer Feel Invisible," Time, Time Inc., June 23, 2015, http://time.com/3932378/gay-marriage-children/

4   Ariel Chesler, "What's Law Got to Do With It? A Straight Married Guy's Perspective on Marriage," HuffPost, MultiCultural/HPMG News, last updated February 2, 2016, https://www.huffingtonpost.com/entry/whats-law-got-to-do-with-it_b_3047129.html

5   Ariel Chesler, "Heather Barwick, Don't Let Your Pain Hurt Other Kids," HuffPost, Multi-Cultural/HPMG News, last updated February 2, 2016, https://www.huffingtonpost.com/entry/heather-barwick-dont-let-_b_6925068.html

I AM NOT AN ALLY

JENNY GANGLOFF RAI, age 47

I AM NOT AN ALLY. No children of LGBTQ+ parents are. We're too inescapably linked to the orientation and gender identities of our parents to remain at the safe distance that allies can. To label us as "only an ally" in the LGBTQ+ narrative is to erase the roads we have walked hand-in-hand with our LGBTQ+ parents. The very word—*ally*—disconnects us from the struggle and paints over the anguish, the coming-out-ness, the wrestling with our own identity and family structure, and the joy of being one "with" our parents. The label *"ally"* minimizes the intimate connection we have with our LGBTQ+ parents.

We are not allies. Though we may stand in this place for now, because we have been granted no other location within the LGBTQ+ narrative, don't mistake us as being as separated from the fight as an ally is. No, we are not separate, we are simply kids who happen to have LGBTQ+ parents and like our LGBTQ+ parents, the ostracism that our parents have experienced, we have too. Many of us for decades. As LGBTQ+ millennials step into the movement and rail against the prejudice that continues to happen in our community, those of us who came of age in the 1970s, '80s, and '90s remember when our families got death threats simply for coming out. We remember the beatings, the hiding, and the mistaken diagnoses of our families as "abnormal" by the psychological and faith communities. We witnessed the horrors of reparative therapy devastating and taking the lives of our parents' friends. We remember when our dads were blamed for AIDS. We remember when the freedoms that the younger generation now take for granted *were taking our families' very lives*.

We remember how our lives were defined by a debilitating shame and ruled by a permeating voicelessness that infected our developing identities.

It was 1981 and my mom had shipped me off from the Midwest to spend the entire summer with my dads in D.C. One of our favorite vacation spots was Rehoboth Beach, Delaware. It was not as commercial as Ocean City, and it was more family-friendly if you happened to be gay. I took to the water from a young age and loved to splash and float about in the ocean waves. The beach had a calming effect on me, and because our vacations to Rehoboth were filled with laughter, I learned to associate the beach with fun, relaxation, and bonding time with my family. Papi and Dencil usually hadn't finished packing our beach bags and I was already out the door climbing into the car, ready to go.

The long Rehoboth days would find Papi, Dencil, and me at the beach sunning and swimming, followed by a quick trip back to our hotel to clean up. Our evenings would wrap up with time plodding down the board-walk in our flip-flops—shopping, eating ice cream, and laughing. I loved boardwalk-time because Papi and Dencil let me go into all of the shops to find #allthethings an eleven-year-old girl loves, like rainbow bouncy balls, grape Pixy Stix, sugar rock candy, Rehoboth Beach magnets, red plastic coin purses that popped open when you squeezed them just right, and pink T-shirts with glitter-colored iron-on decals. Iron-on decals were a big deal in the 80s. They were especially cool on pink shirts. When the iron-on had glitter—glitter *is* considered a color to an eleven-year old girl—it was a trifecta of perfection. We would walk through the stores and laugh at the funny sayings on the shirts. Dencil would find one that Papi "had to get" and it almost always said something about being grumpy. Then we would double over in boisterous laughter while the store clerks glued the iron-on decal with glitter to my new pink shirt.

I was an only child to Papi and Dencil. I was quiet, cooperative, and most days I did what I was told. But when we neared the boardwalk or a strip mall, I transformed into a shopping maven and bee-lined into and out of stores with purpose. If an object presented itself as shiny, pink, or glittered, I wanted it. If it was trendy or if you could only get it at the beach or in D.C., I found a way to talk Papi and Dencil into it. Papi's best defense against "the ask" I had mastered was the response, "We'll see." He thought I knew that meant "no." Since my communication skills have always struggled at the point of interpretation, I decoded Papi's "we'll see" as a "not yet, Jenny. You need to find a better marketing strategy for 'the ask'," or "Papi's blood sugar is low, so let's get him some ice cream and ask him again later." It wasn't until *years* later that I discovered Dencil's affinity for shopping, at which point the two of us schemed together on my poor dad with "the ask." Did I mention both Dencil and I have careers in marketing?

One night we were walking along the boardwalk back to our hotel. I was on the end closest to the ocean so I could hear the roar and pound of the surf against sand and see the occasional shooting star in the ink-black sky. Papi and Dencil were walking next to each other talking. A group of teenage boys had slung themselves over a fence next to the boardwalk on the side farthest from the ocean. Some were sitting on the fence and others were leaning. Because I was nearer to the ocean and the teenage boys were on my far side, perhaps they did not see me. But I heard them.

"Hey, faggot! Hey, gay boys!" they slurred. "Fag boy!" they hissed and sneered.

A couple of them hopped off the fence after taking long drags from their cigarettes and followed behind us, whistling epithets through tar-stained teeth and inter-mittently grabbing their crotches.

"Faggots," they hissed. "Hey, faggots!"

The teenage boys didn't see me turn my head and stare at them. Nor did they seem harmed by the fire that shot from my eyes. I was powerless. Remote. Silenced, yet forcefully present in a moment I could not escape and that defined me for decades.

Papi and Dencil were talking and remained oblivious to the atmospheric shift that the boys had caused. I looked at my dads, then at the boys, and back to my dads. Eventually I glanced at the ocean and longed for the relief and calming of the waves. But it never came.

Time stood still in that moment for me. Like ice-black marble hands, the comments shoved through my pink-glitter, iron-decaled T-shirt and arrested my heart. The rage inside me seethed like molten lava with no escape valve. Because I did not have words for the abuse, my heart remained frozen while my body boiled, and then I became mute. My face turned to stone and my feet to lead. I wanted to cry, but the tears would not come. They were locked inside my stone face.

As we approached the stairs to the hotel, Papi asked me a question that to this day I can't remember. Even if I could remember the question, I had gone mute, so was unable to answer or even acknowledge that a question had been asked. Dencil dismissed my muteness as "typical eleven-year-old-girl stuff" and we continued walking up the stairs. Me as a frozen, lead-footed mute, and Papi and Dencil continuing to plan the next day.

I just wanted to breathe again.

THAT MOMENT MARKED the beginning of my battle with shame. The hateful slurs that targeted my family that night communicated to me that there was something deeply wrong with *me* and something deeply wrong with my *family*. The words told me my family was so unworthy of respect that we *deserved* to be the recipients of hurtful words thrown at us. Shameful words that hurt my developing heart more than fists ever could have. Words that I was too young to understand and was powerless to defend myself against. Words that scarred the landscape of my soul as impermeable carved etchings that were neither pretty, nor unforgettable.

My family wanted to walk along the boardwalk that evening like we always did when we went to the beach, but those teenage boys turned it into a shame battlefield that left my heart and emotions a tattered, bloody mess.

That is the last year I can remember going to Rehoboth Beach. I'm sure we went, but since my security had long departed, the journey was never the same.

AFTER YEARS OF psychology classes, I now know that evening became stored in my brain as a trauma memory that remained "stuck" and unprocessed. My inability to process the complex field of emotions, circumstances, thoughts, and moral implications that occurred that night was because my brain had not yet developed the capacity for that level of reasoning.

At ages ten to eleven, I was in what Piaget called the "Concrete Operational Stage." During this stage of a child's development, their brain doesn't have the capacity for abstract reasoning, which allows them access to problem-solving skills, enables them to hypothesize (the ability to use "what-if" scenarios that may not be based in concrete reality), and use their metacognition ("the capacity for 'thinking about thinking' that allows adolescents and adults to reason about their thought processes and monitor them").

Children in [the Concrete Operational] stage can . . . only solve problems that apply to actual (concrete) objects or events, and not abstract concepts or hypothetical tasks. Understanding and knowing how to use full common sense has not yet been completely adapted.[2]

That evening on the boardwalk, I experienced the concrete *reality* of teenagers marginalizing my dads with abusive language, but I lacked the cognitive *development* to understand how to process it. *I was handed an adult experience with only the brain of a child as a tool to process through it.* For years, it remained lodged in my brain as a 10-year-old's pain.

Furthermore, Lawrence Kohlberg states that:

> . . . *starting at around age ten, children enter the conventional level [of moral development], where their behavior is guided by the opinions of other people and the desire to conform. At Stage 3, the emphasis is on being a "good boy" or "good girl" in order to win approval and avoid disapproval...*[3]

NOT ONLY DID I *not* have the cognitive capacity to process the abstract experience of that evening, I was *ashamed* at my family's inability to conform to the expectations that the teenage boys had leveled. I drastically wanted to escape the disapproval the teenage boys were hurling at my family, yet an internal conflict raged. While I wanted to flee, I also subconsciously wanted the approval of the teenage boys and then detested myself for desiring their approval. I was overcome with the urge to protect my dads from the hellfire I was about to unleash on the teenage boys, as well as the feeling that I needed to flee from the shame that was caused by not having a "normative" family system (as defined by our society). If *you* are confused, imagine my eleven-year-old mental processing system.

This stage also involves "respecting and obeying authority (of parents, teachers, God) [as] an end in itself, without reference to higher principles."[3] Because I trusted my dads as authorities in my life, I was conflicted about how to navigate the juxtaposition of the boys' abuse with my bonded love to them. To me, the most normal and healthy experience of parental love and partner bonding came from my dads, not the heterosexual couples around me who were all in some stage of divorce, separation, or survival mode.

It was a mix of adult thoughts, emotions, and experiences that I had no idea how to resolve.

This benchmark moment initiated a journey of shame that became my constant companion. I lived in constant fear of being made fun of, of embarrassing myself, and of failing to successfully navigate social situations. I was naturally shy, introverted, and an only child who struggled in social environments with my peers, but that evening at the beach slathered on a layer of thick shame that became a shadow and preceded me into every subsequent social event. From a very young age, I had a deep sense of being different and as a result of that difference, inferior to other children who were my age.

RECENTLY, POPE FRANCIS was asked by a weeping young girl, "Why does God allow these things to happen to us? The children are not guilty of anything."[4] Though she was talking about the atrocities of child trafficking, drugs, and prostitution, I have found myself asking the same questions: "Why, God, would you allow me to be traumatized by the verbal abuse of teenage boys trying to hurt my dads?" And, "Where were you, God, when my school friends were telling the gay jokes about my dads?" And later, "God, why is that pastor calling my dad an abomination?" And much later, "God, when that news magazine says that my dads are living in sin, what does that mean for me as their child? Did you even mean for me to exist?"

The Pope's reply was magnificent and worthy of note to each of us as we pause to reflect on the times we may have unwittingly hurt children of LGBTQ+ parents with hateful words:

> *"She is the only one who has put a question for which there is no answer and she wasn't even able to express it in words but in tears," the Pope told a crowd that organisers said reached 30,000. The pope . . . told those in the crowd that they . . . had to learn to cry with other marginalised and suffering people.*[5]

WHAT HAPPENED TO me at Rehoboth is a microcosm of what has been happening to kids like me for decades. When jokes, hateful slurs, or prejudice occur, the more typical victim of our verbal grenades is the child or family member of an LGBTQ+ person. Children are like Velcro and they pick up on things that the adults around them either don't observe, or are emotionally healthy and mature enough to dismiss. But unlike Velcro that can be "unstuck," a child that does not have the cognitive capacity or moral reasoning to unstick him or herself from the shaming will remain glued to those verbal grenades forever.

THOUGH I WOULD like to believe we have made progress in humanizing our LGBTQ+ brothers and sisters and creating a safe developmental environment for children of LGBTQ+ parents since that fateful day on the boardwalk in Rehoboth beach, sadly, it is not so. The anti-LGBTQ+ slurs that I encountered as a young child and the bullying that is still occurring today are identical twins. Thirty-six years ago, I walked away from that encounter on the boardwalk indelibly scarred from the discriminatory slurs lobbed against Papi and Dencil for being gay. Today, children of LGBTQ+ parents are walking out of churches all over our nation just as irrevocably damaged from hate-speech and bigotry masquerading as theology. The most inflammatory hate-speech is happening from our pulpits and the unintended causalities are the children of LGBTQ+ parents who are bystanders to a war going on between equality and theology that they never asked to be a part of.

Furthermore, people like me wake every morning to a retinue of atrocious stories about LGBTQ+-hate crimes, political maneuvers riddled with inflammatory quips, and Sunday sermons where the litmus test of whether a pastor is "Christian" or not is if he includes gay-bashing sermons in his diet of discipleship. Children cannot help but personalize the news they see, the sermons they hear, and the slurs they witness. It is not an option for children of LGBTQ+ parents to distance themselves from anti-LGBTQ+ hate crimes and rhetoric because we live the reality of discrimination on a daily basis. We live with the ever-present reality that when our parents leave the house in the morning, it may be the last time we see them. Wherever LGBTQ+ hate and bigotry is left unchecked, we must bear the burden of fear over the potential loss of our parents.

Though the following statement is made about LGBTQ+ individuals, I believe that it applies to kids of LGBT+ parents as well: "Gay people often know they're "different"" when they are very young—way before they even relate that difference to sexuality."[6]

I not only understood my dads as "different" but I saw myself as "different" too. I was inexorably linked to the experiences of my dads. Difference, shame, and hiding were my response to the discriminatory language and bigotry I experienced. My response to marginalization was no different than what I have witnessed from others in the LGBTQ+ community.

Vicarious trauma is the emotional residue of exposure that counselors experience from working with people as they are hearing their trauma stories and becoming witnesses to the pain, fear, and terror that trauma survivors have endured. I would assert that unicorn kids have experienced vicarious trauma, as we have witnessed our parents being maligned in the media, in churches, and in society. I know because I am still untangling the knotted rope of anti-LGBTQ+ theology and societal hatred that was handed to me as a child. I was gifted with loving dads, but society told me that we were an abnormality and as such, we were okay to dehumanize.

When I hear LGBTQ+ individuals in their early twenties tell me that I have to "earn" my "allyship" I'm left scratching my head at the irony, knowing that, in many cases, the discrimination they have experienced is identical to mine in all manners except duration. We've had similar experiences—I've simply endured them for longer. When I am told that I am "complicit" in the abuse that LGBTQ+ individuals have experienced simply because I am straight, cisgender, and white, I am left with the sense that my own story is not a valid part of the LGBTQ+ narrative. I feel abandoned and erased all over again by the community that I love, that I have suffered for, and that I will continue to fight for—even though they don't recognize my voice. As the child of dads, I can't at once be different from society and different from my LGBTQ+ community. Can I?

ON JUNE 14, 2015—in anticipation of the nationwide marriage equality victory—my story, "How Kids Became the Strongest Argument for Same-Sex Marriage,"[7] appeared on the cover of the *Washington Post*. My testimony was included on page twenty-one of Family Equality Council's Amicus Brief entitled "Voices of Children" and I was conveniently local, so the *Washington Post* sent a reporter and photographer to my house during a violent thunderstorm. The next thing I knew, I was on the cover of the *Post* and the picture I took at my dads' wedding nine months earlier was on page two. I was the sole invitee as well as the photographer at my dads' wedding, and that picture took over the above-the-fold space in the newspaper.

When Papi found out, he said, "Now, you aren't going to go and make your old dads role models, are ya?" I laughed and said, "Of course I am!"

I remember feeling so proud in that moment. Years of shame and erasure were eradicated in that season because of the work of organizations like Family Equality

Council, COLAGE, and One Million Kids for Equality who leveraged the voices of children of LGBTQ+ parents to push marriage equality over the finish line, to get my story on the front page of the *Post*, and to make my family valid in the eyes of the state. For the first time, I had a voice, I was no longer powerless, and I had the opportunity to be proud, not ashamed, of my family. After four decades of marginalization, my dads and I had a legitimate place in the societal narrative of family.

My Facebook feed was awash with rainbow and Confederate flags. Both in equal measure. I laughed when I saw the meme "When the Confederates and a Skittles Factory Went to War" because it aptly described what I was witnessing. Everyone had an opinion on what had happened and Facebook was their megaphone. I sat smiling at my desk and "liked" all of the pride flags on my feed.

Papi called me at work as soon as he found out marriage equality passed and we wept together over the phone. "We are a family! Dencil is your step-dad. I thought I'd never see this day!" Papi and I reflected back to their wedding two years earlier and the couple we had met at the California courthouse who had been together for forty-eight years. I wondered if they were celebrating too. I remember thinking how grateful I was for a Supreme Court decision that mandated that my dads could travel across the nation, and if anything happened to them, they had the legal right to be together in the hospital. The fears that held onto me for decades slipped off layer by layer as the realization of what the marriage equality decision *really* meant for our family hit me. Even my biological mom called to congratulate me from the Bible Belt and asked, "Are you happy?" I said, "Yes, I'm happy and relieved." I could hear her smiling over the phone.

In the Amicus Brief I stated,

> *You don't think that a simple piece of paper designating your parents as "married" can have a tangible difference on the bond you have with them—but it does. I watched decades of marginalization of my family fall away in the moment that the judge pronounced them as husband and husband.*[8]

I HOLD ONTO hope that kids much younger than I will live in a world where they will never have to experience any Rehoboth boardwalk insults from teenage boys because they have LGBTQ+ parents. A world where we will have a voice in the LGBTQ+ community that goes beyond what is useful for Supreme Court decisions and is regularly valued and inquired about in the fight to eliminate systemic erasure. Where tiny hands and feet and hearts and minds and souls are given into the care of two dads or two moms, bisexual or transgender families, and sprung free from the cage of foster care. Where LGBTQ+ parents can leave for work in the morning and be valued, not ashamed of their orientation or gender identity, and return safely home at night to their kids. A world where rainbow families of all stripes and sizes can gather, parents and grandparents with their kids and grandkids around a hospital bed, to bid their loved one goodbye without having to fight the hospital administration for the right to be in the room in the first place simply because a member of their family is LGBTQ+.

This is the world I believe in, that I have fought for, that I have bled for, and will continue to hope for. It is why I do not consider myself a distant ally, but a unicorn kid, divinely fitted together with a strength of purpose and a hard-won voice, rare but cherished, and important in bringing my dream to pass.

1　Jeffrey Jensen Arnett, *Adolescence and Emerging Adulthood*, (New Jersey: Person Education Inc., 2013), 64–65.

2　"Piaget's theory of cognitive development," Wikimedia Foundation, last modified February 7, 2018, 21:22, http://en.wikipedia.org/wiki/Piaget%27s_theory_of_cognitive_development

3　"Lawrence Kohlberg," Net Industries, http://psychology.jrank.org/pages/362/Lawrence-Kohlberg.html

4　Stoyan Zaimov, "Pope Francis Asked by Girl: Why Does God Allow Children to Experience Drugs, Prostitution?," The Christian Post Inc., CMC, last modified January 19, 2015, 13:35, http://www.christianpost.com/news/pope-francis-asked-by-girl-why-does-god-allow-children-to-experience-drugs-prostitution-132780/

5　"Weeping Philippine girl challenges pope on prostitution," Yahoo!, last modified Jnauary 18, 2015, http://news.yahoo.com/weeping-philippine-girl-challenges-pope-prostitution-064923640.html

6　Susan Cottrell, "To a Church That Dehumanizes Gays," Patheos, last modified January 19, 2015, http://www.patheos.com/blogs/freedhearts/2015/01/19/to-a-church-that-dehumanizes-gays-2/

7　Sandhya Somashekhar, "How kids became the strongest argument for same-sex marriage," The Washington Post, last modified June 24, 2015, https://www.washingtonpost.com/politics/how-kids-became-the-strongest-argument-for-same-sex-marriage/2015/06/24/98955632-18fe-11e5-ab92-c75ae6ab94b5_story.html?utm_term=.a3b945d8e76f

8　James Obergefell, et al. and Brittani henry, et al. v. Richard Hidges, Director Ohio Department of Health, et al., Nos. 14-556, 14-562, 14-5871 and 14-574, U.S. App. (6th Cir.), https://www.americanbar.org/content/dam/aba/publications/supreme_court_preview/BriefsV5/14-556_amicus_pet_fec.authcheckdam.pdf

ONE COIN, TWO SIDES

PERSIS TICKNOR-SWANSON, age 21
CALVIN TICKNOR-SWANSON, age 19

LGBTQIA. THERE ARE so many acronyms, phrases, and words to represent this community, it's dizzying. Then there are the sub-communities—twinks, bears, femmes, etc. But amongst all of that, there is no "C" for Children—the children of this community.

Decades ago, the "children" category was not entirely relevant. It only recently became legal in some places for same-sex couples to marry and have joint custody of children. Before that, everything was shrouded in secrecy. Culturally, non-heterosexual couples are now becoming much more common and accepted. As the LGBTQ+ community gains legal rights, some leave the fringe culture that many of the our members inhabited and start to do what many heterosexual couples do: get married. Have a baby. Have multiple babies. Own a house. Raise a family.

This is not a story full of discrimination, hardship, and bullying. I (Persis) do not have many stories to tell that reveal the ugly but unsurprising nature of homophobia. I am a functional, happy, healthy, fairly mainstream member of society. These are stories about family. Families, really. Many of my stories are not uncommon. Mother/daughter conflict, sibling fights, divorce, the struggles of blending families. But mine are unusual enough for the reason that I am part of a growing demographic of children/people without their own letter in an acronym.

As stated, my stories are not full of dramatic pain and struggle, but there *is* a certain level of emotional hardship that I have encountered. The aim of this story is to expose the subtler challenges and contradictions of my experience being raised in a nontraditional family. I want to get at the unseen and intangible forces that shaped my childhood. If I can understand the complex influences I grew up with, I can better understand my own place in the world. So, at the very least, writing this benefits me, if no one else.

Before I introduce you to my family and my emotional world, some disclaimers. I speak for myself and my experiences only. There are innumerable people in comparable situations, and I cannot pretend to speak for this community beyond myself. I also come from a unique and privileged background. I am a white, cisgendered, straight, upper-middle class, college-educated, able-bodied, twenty-one-year-old female. I was raised in a very liberal and wealthy area with bountiful colleges and good schools. I am aware of how lucky I was to grow up in that environment and of the many ways it benefits me.

I mention my brother quite often and some of these stories revolve around him. I do not want to speak for him or pretend to know how any of this affected him.

For me, the stories of witnessing his experiences are just as important as the stories that I am at the center of because they shape my perception of the community I grew up in. As an older sister who absolutely loves and feels close to her brother, his experiences hold important sway over my own emotional memory. I hope this helps to clarify and provide context for the memories I will share with you. Please read his story after mine, as you can hear it directly from his point of view.

PEOPLE ARE OFTEN confused by my family structure unless I explicitly explain my family history. I am not *"Heather Has Two Mommies,"* but I am also not *"The Berenstain Bears."* So here goes.

My mother Estey met my father Swanee in the early 1990s at a boarding school where they both worked. She was a hockey coach, a gym, psychology, and health teacher, and a dorm parent. He was a soccer coach, a history and philosophy teacher, and also a dorm parent. They had a sweet romance. He wrote her love letters. They married in the school chapel.

When they met, he was in his late forties and a bachelor whose mother still stocked his freezer with frozen casseroles. He came from a working class New England family with Swedish immigrant heritage. He had attended this boarding school, came back to teach after college, and never left. She was in her mid-thirties and had moved from eastern Massachusetts to work at this boarding school. She came from a very WASPy New England family with lots of Harvard history and Mayflower connections. She went to Dartmouth College to play hockey and soccer, got a Masters in nutrition, was a bodybuilder at one point, and played on the U.S. Women's National Hockey team.

I was born first in 1995. A girl they named Persis Maida, for my mother's sister and my father's mother. Blond and blue-eyed. In 1998, my brother followed. Calvin August, for my mother's step-grandfather and my father's grandfather. Also blond and blue-eyed.

When I turned five, my parents separated. One of my earliest memories is of them telling Calvin and me they were separating and taking us out for ice cream at Tasty Top. I do not remember what my reaction was to that announcement. I do remember that my parents never fought, at least not in front of us. From what my mother has told me, I know that I struggled with this for years. Now I feel very rational about it, because I understand why it happened and how it turned about to be a good thing for our whole family.

My mom moved to a house in the same town, and my dad helped her move. He stayed in the house that he was given as Dean of Students on the boarding school campus. Calvin and I spent Tuesday nights and some weekends with him and the rest of the time with our mom. My mom went to Boston College to become a social worker, my dad wrote a book about being Dean of Students, and we went to family therapy, the four of us. I talked a lot in therapy and drew obvious pictures about my feelings consisting of angry red scribbles over stick figure images of my mom. My brother quietly played with Legos and made infrequent but insightful high-pitched comments.

I do not recall my mom coming out as a lesbian. Someone asked me recently and I realized I never thought about it, because in most of my conscious memories, she was always queer. She cut her hair short. She started dating a woman named Grace, who had separated from her husband and come out around the same time.

Eventually they broke up and Mom met Julie. Julie had a son named Avery who was nine months older than I was. They started dating when I was seven. We took a family vacation to a resort in Jamaica, and I can remember playing Power Rangers with Calvin and Avery under the supervision of Louisa, our Jamaican nanny.

Blending our two families was not easy. Admittedly, I was an intense child with a lot of feelings and opinions, so Julie and I did not always get along. I was not sure how I felt about having an older stepbrother. More accurately, in the beginning I was rather angry and vicious about it, but eventually I became very attached to Avery. I'm sure there is a lot of emotional history I can talk about here, but I honestly don't remember all of it. I do recall the house my mom and Julie built together, a big one with a pool. I had a room painted light blue. There were holographic fish tiles in the master bathroom. We moved there when I was in fifth grade, after living at my mom's little house together for a year. We adopted a puppy, Baci—my mom's third child.

That family had serious highs and lows. Julie and I had a lot of conflict. She and I fought frequently, which caused me and Mom to fight as well. I don't remember what all the fights were about, but after each fight I vowed through bitter tears that I would stay mad at Mom or Julie, or both, forever. I almost always forgave them within a day.

It was *hard* to have a stepmother, a mother, a father,

and two brothers. This could have been a function of age, as I was a preteen who experienced emotions very intensely and often with obvious manifestations, like saying the cruelest things I could think of to the people around me. But I think navigating complicated family structures is also just difficult, and for whatever reason it was especially so for me.

Still, when they separated, I was fifteen and became heartbroken. Julie and Avery had been my family since I was very little. I loved Avery as my brother. Although Mom and Julie never married, it was essentially a second divorce in my fifteen years.

Again, there is a lot I could say here. Family drama shapes a person deeply. The point is, though, none of it really had anything to do with the fact that my mom was queer. No matter the gender or sexuality of my parents, it still would have been painful, difficult, powerful, and influential.

After Julie, Mom moved Calvin, the dog, and me back to the first town we lived in, five minutes from my dad. She had a couple of less serious girlfriends. When I was eighteen and in my first semester of college, she met Tara. Tara is in her mid-forties and a doctor at a major hospital in our area. She is Indian and Irish and grew up in the Midwest. She met Mom through mutual friends, and Tara quickly became a member of our family.

I am twenty-one now. My brother and I are both in college. My mom and Tara just finished renovating part of our house. My dad and Tara are friends. We celebrate Christmas and birthdays together. My dad dog-sits for Baci when my mom and Tara go on vacation. My mom and dad are in many ways partners when it comes to parenting Calvin and me. We feel like one big family, with smaller units within it.

On Saturday, June 3, 2017, Tara had a baby, a girl named Freddie—my legal half sister—who is twenty-one years younger than me.

Confusing, right? There is a running joke in my family that there should be a TV sitcom about us—and I'm proud of that. I like that I've had an unusual family life. I feel that all the strangeness and confusion and difficulty in my family has shaped me into a strong and resilient woman.

Hearing homophobic bigots argue that non-heterosexual couples should not raise families because they feel it is detrimental to children really boils my blood. There are many things that are injurious to children. Abuse, neglect, poverty, and lack of education are just a few. But terrible things happen to children in all types of families. There are certain groups that are probably more predisposed to suffer from these types of hardships. But the gender and sexuality of parents do not on their own cause children harm. There are bad parents everywhere, of every color, class, gender, and ethnicity. I'm sure there are also bad LGBTQ+ parents. But being gay does not automatically make a parent bad. I truly believe that my childhood was much better because my mother came out. Happy parents are better for their children than unhappy parents. Being queer makes my mother happy, which makes me happy. I would not change a thing about my big, messy, queer, and unique family.

WHEN MY MOTHER came out and started dating Julie, our family began taking our summer Cape Cod trip to

Provincetown instead of Chatham. I refer to P-Town as "the gay male capital of the East Coast." It was my first major exposure to the queer community and it was normalized for me before I was even conscious of it. It was not the most family-friendly place when we started going, but that didn't matter to me.

As a child, particularly a little girl, I was exempt from participating in or being a subject of the culture of sexuality that was constantly visible and performed. Although it was sometimes clear that little children were out of place among the many childless gay men, mostly Calvin and I inhabited an easy role in P-Town, because we were either ignored to the benefit of our freedom or we were fawned over for being a rarity. For us, being children in Provincetown was special. We felt special because we were rare, because we were granted certain physical freedoms, because we were part of something taboo, and because we were too young for our sexuality and gender to be judged and categorized. At least, I was.

The movie *High School Musical* came out in 2006, when I was ten and my brother was eight. We were *obsessed*. The dancing, the singing, Zac Efron as Troy Bolton. It was an absolute inspiration to two little kids who loved dancing and singing. That summer, Calvin got a little outfit to wear from the girls' section of Target: a white T-shirt and gray shorts, both with Troy Bolton's smiling face displayed on them. One of the more adorable moments of his life, in my opinion. One day during our annual summertime P-Town vacation, he wore it out while our family took a stroll down Commercial Street, the very crowded and colorful main drag in the town. There he was, a little eight-year-old with white-blonde hair and a dancer's walk. I remember a gay man stopping and exclaiming to Calvin, "Oh, my, aren't you adorable! I think you have a future here!" Then he winked at my mother. I remember feeling proud of how charming my little brother was, but also indignant. Indignant because even my ten-year-old mind had some understanding that the notion of imposing sexuality on a person because of their choice of clothes was shallow and presumptuous.

When I think about this incident now, I feel it is unusual in a couple of ways and I would dare to assert that parts of it have to do with our mother's queerness. What my mother was doing for us was just being a good mother, regardless of her sexuality. Of course, it is also impossible to truly parse out which aspects of our childhood were influenced by our mother's queerness and the culture we grew up in or by my and Calvin's characters. I believe the contrast in our experiences is essential in understanding how growing up in a queer community is inextricably tied to an individual's expression of gender and sexuality.

My mom's own struggles with her gender expression and sexuality heavily informed how she chose to raise us. Although she came out as queer in her forties, she had been crossing gender boundaries since she was a little kid. The stories she has told me about wanting the cowboy costume her brother Tickie had rather than a cowgirl costume, or the football uniform, or playing hockey with all the boys, all carry obvious significance for her. She did not want us to have to struggle with the same imposed gender stereotypes. We would always have the option between the dress and the pants.

Perhaps this is more obvious in Calvin's case. There

were not very many boys we knew who were dancers and loved *High School Musical*. But Calvin and I had never been entirely gender-conforming. This was probably partially a result of our mother actively encouraging us to buck gender norms, or more subtly being careful about imposing gender stereotypes on us. It could also be the result of some intrinsic qualities we possessed. I was a fairly aggressive and powerful little girl, and Calvin was a sensitive and caring little boy. We each had various types of transgressions surrounding gender, but it was more obvious for Calvin.

I grew up in the post-Title IX world where little girls were encouraged to play sports and were told they could do anything the boys could do. But boys were not receiving the same message. In fact, it was often firmly the opposite: boys were not encouraged to participate in activities considered girly, like dancing and playing with dolls, or emulate traditional girly behavior, such as crying or expressing affection. There were often painful social punishments for boys that crossed these boundaries. Increasingly, there is now an awareness that the culture of masculinity can be toxic to boys. While girls in my cohort were being told they could do anything by their progressive teachers and parents, the boys were still receiving the same messages about gender and sexuality that their parents received. Act tough. Don't cry. Don't like dolls, or pink, or babies, or playing house.

Calvin did not receive these messages, at least not from my mother. He had as many American Girl dolls as I did. He played dress up with me and we would perform dance parties and fashion shows for our parents after dinner. All of his closest friends were girls.

He was encouraged to talk about his feelings and to cry. Once, when he was around three years old, he was running around my uncle Tickie's kitchen with all the cousins. While trying to keep up with his older cousins, he stopped in the middle of a lap and in his breathless little-boy voice, turned to my uncle Tickie unprompted and said, "It's okay to cry, Tickie, it's okay to cry!" and then took off again. This is a favorite story among our extended family because it says a lot about both Calvin and Tickie. At such a young age, Calvin had a developed emotional awareness and was attempting to communicate a message he had probably received from our mom to his uncle: that it was okay for a boy to cry.

All of this is relevant to understanding why wearing a girl's outfit with Troy Bolton's face was not something strange for Calvin to do in our family. To me, because of the open environment my mother encouraged around gender expression, Calvin was just being Calvin. He also happened to love trucks, monsters, gross things, bothering his sister, running around, getting dirty, and aliens. Calvin and I both received the message that we could do or like anything we wanted, no matter which gender that activity was associated with.

Gender expression has always been very tightly associated with sexuality. They used to be linguistically indistinguishable. When that gay man on the street predicted Calvin's "future" in P-Town, implying that he would return some day as a gay man, he was continuing that practice. Feminine gender expression must mean attraction to men. Although considering the possibility of being gay was a kind of openness in its own right, it still involved subscribing to a limited notion of gender and sexuality. Effeminate men must be gay. Gender-bending little boys will end up gay. Or trans-gendered.

It is significant to me that the gay man in P-Town commented on Calvin's gender expression and sexuality rather than mine. I was a little girl, and therefore could never gain full access to the world of gay men in P-Town the way my brother could. Because he was a boy who crossed the rigid accepted boundaries of expressed boyhood, his sexuality and gender expression were highlighted and analyzed. Even in the LGBTQ+ culture of transgression, Calvin was still subjected to the performance rules of gender expression and sexuality when he was merely eight.

Although my mother encouraged a radical freedom of expression, she had introduced us to a new culture, the LGBTQ+ one, that had its own rules and stereotypes about expression of gender and sexuality. So while she had attempted to prevent expectations of gendered expression, considerations of sexuality and gender became nearly constant in our lives in some form or another. I don't think this negatively influenced either Calvin or me in any permanent way. What it did was develop our awareness of gender performance, and help us develop a conscious awareness of how gender and sexuality play out in the world around us.

The first time that *my* gender and sexuality were scrutinized and acknowledged in P-Town, I was eighteen years old. I had finally been able to bring my high-school boyfriend to one of the places most special to me. I was so excited to show him the vibrant world of P-Town through my eyes, as a girl who thought herself a part of that community rather than a normal, straight, Cape Cod tourist who made the trip for the day. We were walking down the street, hand in hand, and a carload full of young gay guys drove past. One catcalled out at us, playfully wagging his finger at our interlocked hands, "Uh, uh, uh! None of that here!" They all laughed, and my boyfriend and I giggled, too. I understood the tease, but suddenly for the first time, I felt like an outsider in the community that I had always cherished as my own. I realized I could no longer pass in the category of a little girl without a sexuality or gender. It was no longer obvious that I was the child of a queer vacationing in P-Town, wearing her Carnival T-shirt and walking her rainbow-collar-clad dog with the confidence of a person who had navigated those packed cobbled streets since she was seven. In that moment, I had entered a P-Town category that I had never previously occupied: straight girl. After that, I often felt the urge, and sometimes I still do, to blurt out to gay men or lesbians or queers, "I'm not a regular straight girl, I have a queer mom!" I want to justify my place in that town, my membership in that community.

I am sure many girls remember moments in their life where someone called attention to their gender or sexuality. I had my own variations of these moments in the general world. There was the time a truck driver blatantly stared at my oblivious twelve-year-old downy legs stretched out on the dashboard of my mother's car until she made a face at him. Or the time a boy my age at a bar mitzvah saw me dancing and told my stepbrother Avery that he thought I was cute, making me blush and realize I thought he was cute, too. But I had the unique experience of coming into my sexuality in a community defined by sexuality. And I happened to identify as pretty much the one identity not included in that acronym: straight. Which left me wondering where, and if, I belonged in a community I had grown up in.

When Calvin and I walk down the streets of P-Town now, I'm sure people draw a variety of conclusions, particularly if we are not with our mother. We are towheaded, young, and relatively preppy. We look too much alike to be dating, but we are very affectionate and close. I doubt anyone thinks I'm queer, but I am sure Calvin's sexuality gets questioned much more often as an attractive, stylish young man. We could be tourists who came to see the spectacle of gayness on Commercial Street. I could be a sister visiting her gay brother in P-Town.

When we are with our mother and Tara, I feel more relaxed. Safer. Like I am carrying my passport to the LGBTQ+ community. I am not just a straight girl; I am a child of this community.

"See!" I want to shout, "I have a queer mom! And she has a girlfriend!" I can go back to comfortably judging the straight families I see wandering around looking slightly shell-shocked by all the rainbows and men kissing and raunchy advertisements. *"Not me,"* I think. *"I am totally comfortable with this community. I was raised in it!"* Calvin and I can joke about our mom and Tara's queerness like we are insiders. We smile and laugh with the gay men my mom and Tara befriend at the Tea Dance.

Figuring out where I live on the identity map of P-Town will be an ongoing project. I do not think it would be the same for me to vacation there without my mom. But I will not give up my membership in that community, either. I may be straight, but my mom isn't, and therefore the LGBTQ+ community will always be a part of my identity.

SOMETIMES I WISH I didn't look like such a straight girl. That yucky feeling didn't start to cross my mind until I was eighteen, when I went college. I attend Barnard College, the all-women, liberal arts school that is an undergraduate college of Columbia University with its own campus and board of trustees. I chose it because it was in New York City, and has a strong academic reputation, rigorous curriculum, and the promise of an empowering community of women within a larger coed university. My utter certainty about my desire to attend Barnard was a surprise to me. For years, I had been aggressively against attending a women's college. That was partially because I grew up so close to Smith College and did not want to be at a small, isolated school. Also, I like boys. I like being friends with them and I like dating and hooking up with them.

Maybe I felt okay with my decision because I had a boyfriend at the time, but we broke up the fall of my freshman year. I hoped that I could still have guy friends and interactions since Columbia was across the street, and that has been true to an extent. It's also possible that part of the reason I felt okay with attending a women's college was that I was comfortable with the lesbian/queer reputation that women's colleges tend to have. I thought to myself, *"I grew up around lesbians. This will be familiar."*

To my surprise and discomfort, it was not. During

New Student Orientation, I met my orientation group. One of the other students was a person who used they/them pronouns and made it clear they were a part of the queer community. I wanted so badly to be friends with them, probably because I hoped they would make me feel closer to the home I was sorely missing. But I realized, painfully, that I was not going to have that moment of acknowledgment, usually unspoken, that we were a part of the same community—the LGBTQ+ one.

I'd had that moment with other children of queers and I'd heard about it and witnessed it many times through my mom. Now, however, there was nothing outwardly about me that would indicate I was part of the LGBTQ+ community. I looked like such a straight girl. Eventually, I found a way to mention that my mom was queer. After that, I'm pretty sure the queer person acted friendlier towards me. Maybe I was imagining it, and they did not care and merely became friendlier because we all got to know each other better, but I still felt relieved that they knew. I had my passport to the LGBTQ+ community and maybe I could get in at this new school with new people.

That never really happened. Even though I am a child of a lesbian, I identify as straight. I cannot claim to share the same emotional background as people who do not identify as straight. At times, I feel ashamed of wanting to be part of this community. How could I, as a straight girl, dare to try to claim a spot in the LGBTQ+ acronym? I hold a privileged position in society as a cisgendered heterosexual. This shame could have been an underlying factor in why I never joined the Gay/Straight Alliance at my high school. It could also be why

I never joined any sort of ally group or Pride group in college. I felt like I did not belong.

I realized my experience as a child was in a far different queer community than the one I encountered at college. The queers and lesbians I grew up with were all from an older generation. They were not my peers. Also, in my experience, they have slightly different views on gender and sexuality than the queer community in my age group does. Usually this means they are less radical. In college, I found that the queer community did not feel familiar or welcoming – there was a different energy. One simple contrast that stood out to me was between the reactions of my peers and the reactions of my parents and their friends to the Supreme Court decision for Obergefell vs. Hodges in 2015, which ruled that marriage is a fundamental right for same-sex couples. My parents' generation was joyful and tearful to have won a victory according them the same rights as straight people. My peers were not entirely satisfied. Some thought that it was not enough to be like straight people and the institution of marriage was rotten anyway.

I am not going to side with one or the other. It's not my purpose to pass judgment on the goals of the LGBTQ+ community. I want to emphasize that I am in the odd place of being more comfortable in the community of the older generation of queers I was raised in rather than with my peers. Maybe the world is different now, and the LGBTQ+ community is becoming more indistinguishable from the mainstream community. I have non-straight friends and non-binary friends. I am open about my support and love for the community. But

I have not joined any groups or clubs about it. I have been to more Pride marches and gay bars with my family than with my friends. I hang out with my parents' queer friends when I am home more than I hang out with my queer friends at school.

Towards the end of freshman year, it became clearer that some of my friends were not straight. Some of my floor-mates started hooking up with each other. My friend from French class made it clear they were queer. I remember feeling excited that I had found people in the LGBTQ+ community that were my friends, not people I knew through my mother. I had made my own connections in the community. One night I texted my mom, "I have lesbian friends now!" And I do. But they are also just my friends. Their sexuality did not really change how I felt about the community and my place in it. I still look like a straight girl and I still sometimes wish I didn't. It's an ongoing project for me, to find where I fit in this community. Maybe I should start a "Children of Queers" club. Maybe I should go to a gay bar with my friends. Maybe I should help advocate for justice for queer youth. At the very least I've now done the classic liberal arts thing and written a personal essay about it.

I OFTEN DANCE around my mom's queerness with friends until they get to know me really well. I'm certain some of this is attributable to lingering embarrassment or anxiety about my mom's queerness from when I was younger, back when my peers used the word "gay" as an insult. I would reference my stepmother without clarifying that she was my mom's partner, not my dad's. When it was finally unavoidable to reveal, I would watch understanding dawn on my friends' faces when I mentioned "my mom's girlfriend." Sometimes people would comment, "Oh, I didn't know your mom was gay!" Sometimes they wouldn't say anything, either out of politeness and a desire to seem casual about it, or out of judgment. I don't have any memories of anyone saying something homophobic in response. Every now and then I am curious to know if my mother's queerness influences how my friends see me or my family. I wonder if they think, "Wow, she's so normal for having gay mom!" or "Oh, I can tell her about my sexuality," or "That's why her mom dresses like a guy." Or, maybe they don't think anything at all.

My failure to be direct about my mother's queerness could also come from my own sense of normalcy about it. As I mentioned at the beginning of this piece, I do not remember a time when my mother wasn't queer. Mostly, her sexuality is irrelevant to the reasons I mention her to my friends. She sends me silly texts or pictures of our dog. She can be super annoying about reminding me of items on my to-do list. She comforts me and assists me when I'm feeling sad, anxious, or stressed. She's just another regular mom, until she isn't. She's queer, wears the same outfits as my brother, has absolutely no understanding of feminine beauty practices, and makes Calvin and me listen to Dan Savage podcasts in the car. Then again, maybe the point is there are lots of moms and dads out there now that don't conform to traditional standards of "mother" and "father." There are lots of kids now with nontraditional parents and families. That's comforting to me, that even if we don't have the letter "C" in the LGBTQ+ acronym, we still exist.

When I think about my brand-new little sister Freddie, I find myself wondering how her family story will be told. She will have the same family, but I'm sure her perspective will be quite different. She will be growing up in a culture that will be twenty years different from the one I grew up in. It's possible there will be a strong community for children with lesbian parents. Alternatively, maybe it will become so normal to have LGBTQ+ parents that children won't feel like there is a difference between themselves and their peers with straight parents. I'm not sure which I would prefer. All I know is that growing up with a queer mom is an aspect of myself that I cherish. I am grateful that I was immersed in a world of love and acceptance. I treasure the memories of attending Northampton Pride with rainbow face paint, making a "pilgrimage" with my mom to the Stonewall Inn to drink cosmos, and spending summers in Provincetown with my family.

My mom used to sing me a song originally by Fred Small and covered by The Flirtations, a gay male a cappella group who sang at my mom and dad's wedding. It is called "Everything Possible" and she would sing it to me when she tucked me in for bed. One of the verses goes,

> *"You can be anybody you want to be,*
> *You can love whomever you will*
> *You can travel any country where your heart*
>   *leads*
> *And know I will love you still*
> *You can live by yourself, you can gather friends*
>   *around,*

You can choose one special one
But the only measure of your words and your
* deeds*
Will be the love you leave behind when you're
* gone"*

I KNOW THAT hearing these words before I truly understood their full meaning was profoundly important to me. My mother was doing all she could to impart to me that my identity would never have to be limited, which I think can be attributed in part to her queerness. But more importantly, she did what any good mother would do: she taught me about love and how to be a good person. And that exists independently of sexuality or gender.

I hope my mom sings this song to Freddie. I hope Calvin sings it to his children. I know I will sing it to my children. My children will learn that my mother sang it to me. And I hope that someday I will be as good a mother to my children as my queer mother was to me.

A reflection on Persis's story, written by her brother, Calvin:

IT'S FUNNY TO think about my experiences of being raised with a queer parent while attending a Lady Gaga concert and going to a gay dance club in Provincetown with my mom, her partner, and my sister. Until reading my sister's above essay, I hadn't ever considered the differences between our experiences of being raised by a queer mom, but they are significant.

Being three years younger than my sister, I remember nothing of the time when my mom was still married to my dad and identified as straight. I have no memories of their divorce or my mom's coming out. I can't even pinpoint a time when she started dating women, although I'm pretty sure I remember her first girlfriend. However, this didn't really make an impression on me, either, because she happened to be the mother of my best friend since birth, so all I focused on was the increased number of playdates I got out of it.

I can barely remember meeting Julie, my mom's first serious, long-term, female-identifying partner. The transition into living as a blended family with Julie and her son Avery doesn't stand out in my mind as being unusual or difficult. I can't recall if I had any feelings about it other than excitement for the big new house we were building, with a *pool*. Also, my room was going to be painted firetruck-red. I'm positive though, that I never had any concerns or negative feelings about having a queer mom and being a part of a nontraditional family. I simply had no preconceptions about, or knowledge of the social and cultural implications of queerness to have reason to.

My viewpoint is partly due to my privilege of being a white male living in the liberal bubble of Western Massachusetts where queerness holds few consequences. But it's also attributed to my upbringing by a queer mom, immersed in the LGBTQ+ community. From a young age, I made no distinction between a gay relationship and a straight one. They were both "normal." The thought never crossed my mind that queerness was considered unconventional or wrong by many people.

Growing up, I did not follow gender expectations. When I was very young, about three or four years old, I would put on my sister's dresses and spin around the living room. I liked how the dresses would fan out and poof up while I twirled. The sensation of being free without the constriction of pants was exciting and satisfying for me. This is just one example of how I didn't follow gender norms. I was not aware of my societal transgressions, though. My mom never told me that boys don't wear dresses. She did her best to raise us without these gender boundaries.

Knowing how difficult it was for my mom growing up as a tomboy but being so often denied the opportunity and means to showcase her masculinity, it makes sense why she strived to give my sister and me the freedom to express ourselves across gender boundaries. Reflecting back on my childhood, I am *so* grateful my mom didn't impose gender norms on either me or my sister. My biggest passion in life thus far is an activity often thought of as too feminine for boys: dance. When I was about four years old, I saw Persis taking ballet class and I wanted to be just like her. I've been dancing for fifteen years since then. If I hadn't been encouraged to break gender norms, I wouldn't be the same person I am today.

I loved going to Provincetown, Cape Cod. In my mind, P-Town was a place where other people were doing what I was doing. Everyone was dressing in fun outfits and being performative. The fact that it was mostly men was inspiring to me. It reinforced and affirmed my expression of femininity and masculinity. It had nothing to do with sexuality. That story about the gay man telling me I had a future in P-Town had no connotation to me other than I embodied the aesthetic of the place. I was too young to understand his implications, and if I could've, I wouldn't really have cared. Aesthetic was more important for me; it wasn't about gender or sexuality. I just liked looking good and having fun.

Up until middle school, when I was about twelve years old, I had little worry of discrimination towards my mom or me. Middle school was when I started to become aware of the stigma. It was the first time I ever heard anyone use the word "gay" as an insult and the first time I heard someone say "faggot." It was a rude awakening. I started to have hesitations about telling people my mom was queer. I would be embarrassed when she came to Parent's Day and shameful at the same time for even having those thoughts about the woman I loved most in the world.

I think some of those feelings came from my newfound worry about people thinking I was also gay. Being a sensitive and shy boy, I desperately wanted to fit in and be liked. The idea that being non-heterosexual was not cool started to influence my behavior. For me, gender expression did not equal sexuality. In middle school, I found out that other people did equate the two, so I tried to change. I dressed more masculine, I played more sports and stopped dancing for a year. I even tried to deepen my voice. My attempts to change how I expressed my gender were pointless, though, because after two years of unsuccessfully pretending I was someone I wasn't, I realized that I'd stopped caring. If dancing made me happy, then I would continue to do it no matter if people thought I was gay or a pussy or whatever. I knew who I was, and that's all that mattered to me.

Here I am now, a nineteen-year old student at Northwestern University where I am surrounded by an accepting community of people of all different types of identities. A large portion of my peers identify as something other than straight, and some even identify as gender non-binary. Being raised in the LGBTQ+ community, I feel very comfortable around these people. Probably more so than I do around straight people— men in particular. Members of this community often break the mold of gender expression, like me, or at least are more accepting of it.

I'm not saying I'm exceptionally uncomfortable around straight or heteronormative people—that is certainly not the case. I just can't always relate to the stereotypical masculinity of some straight men. Additionally, discoveries I have made about my own sexuality have altered my relationship to the queer community. I don't consider myself straight or gay. Truthfully, I don't really like to put a label on my sexuality because I'm tired of the assumptions and expectations that come along with them. I find many people attractive: women, men, etc.

Why should I confine myself to a particular category when I can't say any of them feel right? I'm a human with opinions and feelings that change every day. Isn't that enough? On top of that, I no longer feel the need to exude masculinity in my style and behavior. I've moved past that middle school mindset. In fact, I've returned to my pre-adolescent notions of holding aesthetic and pleasure over gender expression and reinforcement. Some people might look at me and assume I'm straight, some people might assume I'm gay. The point is, I'm Calvin, and that's all that should matter.

My mother raised me immersed in a community that values individual expression regardless of gender expectations and sexuality identity. Yes, she taught me a lot that helped me understand and be comfortable with my sexuality and gender expression, something a non-queer parent might do very differently. But, more importantly, as my sister said, she taught me how to live truthfully and be a good person, just like any parent should. My experience just involved a lot more rainbows.

LEARNING TO DANCE

KATE HILLYER, age 43

MY MOM ALWAYS says that the first time she danced with another woman, her immediate thought was, "I'm going to have to get another divorce." It was the 1970s, and she, in her second marriage, was a stay-at-home mom to my brother and me, then seven and three. She went to the lesbian bar on a lark when some neighbors in our apartment building invited her. It was a chance to get out of the house and try something new and different. When a woman asked her to dance, she thought it would be rude to say no. But as soon as she felt the woman's arms around her, as they swayed to the music in that dim and smoky bar, her life changed forever.

She divorced my father within a year. She had no income, but didn't press my father for child support because her attorney had advised that she would lose custody of us if the case ever made it to a judge. Instead, she found a cheap basement apartment and a job as a waitress. What I remember from that time is that she worked almost constantly. In the middle of the night when she returned home, I would cling to her, her warmth the comfort I craved with a weepy desperation.

After a few months, she found a better job, in an office, and a row house in the city. Her face relaxed, and she laughed more. Then Janice began to come around. Janice looked a little like my mom, with short, dark hair and a medium build, but she had the easy manner of one with few responsibilities. She was young, just twenty-six years old, and fascinated by my brother and me. She asked us real questions, and listened to our answers, showing not a glimpse of waning attention as I regaled her with tales of Strawberry Shortcake and ballerina fairies. Sometimes, today, people ask what I thought about my mom dating a woman. In truth, there was nothing to think about. It didn't seem strange or problematic. She was an adult who read to me, and nothing else really mattered at the time.

Eventually, Janice moved in with us. The house, in the inner city of Wilmington, Delaware, was rundown but lovely, with a wide wooden staircase and cut-glass doorknobs that I imagined were real diamonds. I got my own bedroom, which my parents painted pink for me, with a white dresser that had little pink roses on the knobs. At night, Mom and Janice would sit on the end of the bed and read to me from *Little Women* and *The Secret Garden*.

Our rambling old house was soon filled with batik prints, Holly Near songs, and a tumbling array of women with short hair, glasses, and overalls. Suddenly I had "aunties" around, who took me to the park and taught me about art and science and literature. And gay men! I loved when they showed up, because they always brought me extravagant stuffed animals or fancy dresses.

There were pets, too. Janice came with dogs, and in the new house, my brother and I each got a kitten. Both cats got pregnant at the same time, and for a brief and glorious time our house held two moms, two kids, two dogs, two cats, and eleven kittens.

My parents, good 1970s lesbian feminists, tried mightily to raise us free of gender stereotyping. This was the era of "Free to Be You and Me," and Marlo Thomas's idealistic singsong was on heavy rotation in our household. Mom and Janice gave my brother dolls, and gave me a shiny red firetruck. Their efforts were for naught with our cisgendered selves. My brother made nooses and hung his dolls from the coffee table, and I propped my Barbie up on the firetruck and rode her around as if it were the pink Corvette.

They needn't have worked so hard at it, though. Their example was the best demonstration of all that women could do anything that men could. Whatever issue arose in the house, a woman handled it. They cooked, cleaned, gardened, and made household repairs themselves. Janice sanded and repainted our front porch. One Christmas they gave me a dollhouse they'd made over months in the basement, sawing and joining the wood, and decorating it with scraps of carpet and wallpaper.

For the most part, they handled it all smoothly, but there were the occasional Lucy and Ethel moments. Once I woke in the middle of the night to thuds and the sounds of my parents alternately shrieking and laughing. A bat had gotten into the house, and Mom ran through the upstairs screaming and waving a tennis racket overhead. Janice chased her as closely as she dared with an open pillowcase, in the vain hope of trapping it. Finally, it occurred to them that the lights were probably stressing out the poor bat. They switched them off and opened a window, and the bat flew out without incident.

We were one of the sole white families in our predominantly black neighborhood, in addition to being the only one headed by two women, and it was the former fact that loomed larger in my world. I was the only white kid in my kindergarten class, and the girls, curious, would crowd around me and touch my hair, while I sat, stock-still, on the carpet, hoping that if my hair pleased them they might invite me to play. No such luck. They weren't mean, but they were distant, and I struggled to make friends. That I had two moms never came up, but I was so strange and foreign to them that I think they would have viewed it in the same way as if I told them that my parents were circus people, or cosmonauts.

I did have one friend, who was the other white girl in the neighborhood. Wendy was a tough, scrappy redhead with knobby knees and dirty elbows. She and I made up elaborate fantasies of kidnapped princesses who reclaimed their thrones and jewel heists involving the doorknobs, but always at my house, never at hers. To this day, I am not sure what was happening at her house, but I imagine it must have been a lot worse than having two moms.

When I was in fourth grade, we moved to a suburb in Northern Virginia. We had a whole house to ourselves, not connected to any other houses, which I'd never had before. We had also moved into Reagan/ Bush territory. By this time, the general public was gaining more awareness of gays and lesbians. Harvey Milk was elected to the San Francisco City Council in 1977, garnering national prominence as one of the first openly gay elected officials in the country. Representative Gerry Studds came out on the floor of the U.S. Congress in 1983. The emergence of HIV/AIDS in the 1980s brought the gay and lesbian community together, and led to the formation of groups like ACT UP. This emergence prompted a backlash, though, as those who had never considered the possibility of gays and lesbians realized that they might be living among them, and they weren't pleased about that. Of course, I didn't know any of this at the time, though the backlash made itself known to me soon enough.

The first time I was asked the question, the movers were still hauling couches and boxes into the house. My parents occupied, I wandered out into the front yard, where the next-door neighbor collared me. She was a mom—fluffy hair, boring clothes, a saccharine demeanor. I spoke to her dutifully and politely, as I did to all adults. At her prodding, I explained about my dad not living with us, that I had an older brother that one woman was my mom, and the other was Janice.

"And where does Janice sleep?" she asked, in the same sweet and casual manner.

I felt the razor hidden in that question, though I didn't know where. Too young to lie, or even to know why I would, I answered, "She sleeps in the big bedroom."

"And your mother?" she pressed.

I stared at the knees of her pastel pants. "In there, too."

"Uh-huh," she said curtly, and flounced away.

I sensed that I had lost something, messed something up, but I didn't know how or what. When I later recounted the conversation to my parents, they told me, over set jaws and glances back and forth to each other, that I didn't need to answer questions from adults about where they slept, and that if anyone asked, I should say to go ask one of them.

The question would come again—in stores, on beach vacations, at soccer tournaments. Sometimes I tried out their response. It got the same satisfied smirk that I'd gotten when I answered my neighbor truthfully, because those inquiring adults knew what it meant when I wouldn't answer the question. I came to loathe that look, and the cold dismissal that followed.

So, I tried out different answers. Sometimes I obfuscated: "There are three bedrooms upstairs, and my brother sleeps down in the basement." Sometimes I lied, poorly: "She sleeps in the guest room." When I began to tire of the question, I wouldn't answer it, just stare at them until they grew uncomfortable. This was momentarily satisfying, but took a lot out of my generally eager-to-please self. It was easiest to avoid the question in the first place.

And so, over those first few years in Virginia, I learned two things. One was how to steer conversations with strangers away from my moms, and their relationship to one another. I became adept at the game that every queer person knows how to play. I only ever referred to "my parents," not "Mom and Janice." I avoided all pronouns when discussing my parents. I thought three steps ahead in every conversation—*if I mention that I went to the movies last weekend, they'll ask who took me, and I already said that my mom was sick, and so I'll just say it was a fun weekend without mentioning anything specific that I did.*

The second thing I learned was that my parents weren't going to be able to protect me from adults' probing questions. This was something I was going to have to figure out on my own. More challenging was when I had to learn how to hide from my friends.

Amanda Painter was the most popular girl in the fifth grade. Her hair was sleek, blonde, and perfectly feathered. She was just the right mix of kind and cruel, funny and brave, to be pre-teen royalty. If you were friends with her, you were golden, anointed.

I'd been on the edge of her circle for months, and when she invited me to sleep over one Saturday night, I was both thrilled and terrified. This was my big chance. I couldn't mess it up.

I trundled over to her house on the big night. I had the wrong sleeping bag, of course. My parents were lesbians; I had a sturdy camping sleeping bag, not the soft, fluffy kind made for sleeping on carpeted basement floors, like all my friends had. I'd made the argument to them enough at that point to know that it wouldn't work, even if I tried to explain how important Amanda Painter was. Camping sleeping bags were stronger, warmer, and folded up smaller. My parents couldn't see any other consideration for a sleeping bag. I swallowed my pride and carried my sleep sack, tucked behind my overnight bag and pillow, over to Amanda's.

The evening went well enough. We ate pizza and watched a movie. In retrospect, I probably wasn't quite wild enough to hold Amanda's interest, but I was vigilant not to commit error, and I did not. There were no catastrophes, no slip-ups. I was succeeding.

The next morning, I went to church with Amanda's family. It was one of those not-quite-legitimate churches that didn't have a proper building. It met in a school cafeteria, where we sat on folding metal chairs. The air conditioning wasn't turned on over the weekends, so the room was stifling. I fidgeted in my uncomfortable church clothes, and focused on how to impress Amanda without getting her or myself in trouble with her parents. I can't remember the minister, but picture him as a large, balding white man, sweating, in a brown suit.

He delivered the sermon from a podium at the front of the room. It was a fire-and-brimstone soliloquy, so at odds with the cutouts of smiling fruits and vegetables dancing on the walls. The subject was the sin of homosexuality. He alternated raging rhetoric about the doom that would befall all of us, as it did Sodom and Gomorrah, with prancing mockery. His biggest laugh line was, "After all, if God had wanted homosexuality, he wouldn't have made Adam and Eve. He'd have made Adam and Steve!" Guffaws surrounded me.

I froze. Amanda, oblivious, was still making fun of nearby churchgoers. I finally forced a smile and tried, uselessly, to block out the hate pouring over me. By that point, I already knew not to lead with telling friends about my parents. This was the moment that I realized that I needed to hide it. Amanda Painter thought homosexuality was a sin. It was disgusting and unnatural. To be condemned, to be laughed at. And if she, the Queen of Fifth Grade, thought that, so did everyone else.

After that, I was determined that no one should know about my parents. My lies became more planned out, and better. And I succeeded. I became popular. High school for me consisted of football games, fifths of alcohol, and a blurry stream of preppy friends. The thing about popularity is that you have a million friends, and none. I could walk into any classroom on the first day of school and see a few of the fellow anointed, and sit with them, be accepted by them. I never felt left out, in any environment. In a way, I was bulletproof. But as I knew (as I'm sure every popular kid knows), that protection was paper-thin. If I messed up in any way, I could be excommunicated. So, I never told anyone about Janice, not even my closest friends.

My parents, taking their cue from me, stepped back. Janice attended fewer public events. She was "a friend of my mom's" who sometimes showed up on big occasions, like prom photos, but otherwise was conveniently absent. My parents tried, occasionally, to break through, asking if I had any questions about them or their relationship. By then, though, any discussion would have made my daily denial of their love more difficult, and so I always shut those conversations down as quickly as I could.

I had no intention of the situation ever changing. I had reached a balance point, where I could have a stable home, and friends. That my parents happened to be two women had no relevance to the outside world, and thus was none of its business.

And then I went to Smith.

One of the aunties I had known since early childhood had been a professor at Smith College, a liberal women's college in Massachusetts, and my parents put Smith on the college tour in the fall of my junior year of high school. I fell in love with the October explosion of leaf color, the quaint and cozy house system, and the directed and engaged student body. As a high school senior, debating between the University of Virginia and Smith, I felt the pull between life as I knew it, which would be continued on a much more familiar path at UVA, and the unknown possibility of a different path, at Smith. As much as I wanted to cling to the familiar, the heart of me wanted Smith.

My first clue that things were going to be different at Smith was when I walked in the front door of my new house, and saw two women lounging on each other on a couch in the entryway. My mind quickly registered that they were lying too close together to be friends, and thus must be a couple. They clocked us too, and jumped up eagerly to help my moms and me unload our pickup truck.

Word apparently spread fast that I had two moms, and the lesbian community at Smith welcomed me, though respected my reticence about discussing my family. That reticence didn't last long in the friendly environment at Smith, where lesbianism was generally treated with a shrug, and people were more interested in whom you had a crush on than the torment of the coming-out process. At a party one night in late September, over vodka and tears, I finally said the words I'd never said: "My parents are lesbians."

To me, the admission was agonizing. The secret had grown in me, become a part of me, and releasing it had the force of extracting a bullet after the wound had healed over. My confession was met with nonchalance and a little amusement. "I know," my friend said. "I met your moms. And my dad is gay."

Isn't that always the way it is? The secret that we work so hard to maintain is really no secret at all. A year later I told my best friend from high school. I had been terrified to tell her, because she'd been active in Young Life, a Christian group, for many years. We sat on a metal cot in a dorm room at her college and I again agonized over the words. "I just—what I never said—about my mom and Janice—"

"That they're together?" she interrupted. "Of course I knew. I was at your house all the time. How could I not? But you never wanted to talk about it, so I didn't bring it up."

"What about Young Life?" I asked.

"Young Life is whatever," she said, flicking her hand to mime shooing away a troublesome fly. "You're my best friend."

Back at Smith, I had more revelations to confront. That friend to whom I initially came out about my moms ended up being my first girlfriend. It turns out I'd been struggling so hard to deny my parents' sexuality that I hadn't even considered my own. For the first time in my life, I felt what others had described—a drop in my stomach every time she entered a room. A sudden preoccupation with what my hair looked like when I ran into her. An irrational desire to be with her, all the time. One advantage I had as the daughter of lesbians was that it was harder for me to deny these feelings. It was a crush, and I knew it.

Late that fall, without any planning, I came out to my mom on a phone call home. I should mention at this point that my mom is a newspaper reporter. It's really hard to keep anything from her. Over the course of our call, she got out of me that I hadn't been sleeping well, and wasn't eating much.

"What's going on?" she asked, in her characteristic blend of gentle and firm.

I squirmed, but couldn't dodge a pointblank question, not from my mom. "Well, I think I...I kind of have a crush on Dawn," I stammered. It was so embarrassing. I had never discussed romantic feelings of any kind with my mom.

She paused for just a moment. "Oh. Well, that is hard." She advised me to take care of myself, rest, try to remember to eat. She said that I didn't have to make any huge decisions. Just take one step at a time, she said, and follow your heart. When we got off the phone, I felt lighter, and so happy.

To me, she was a model of support. Secretly, to each other, my parents wrung their hands. "Is it something we did? Is it Smith? Is it a phase?" After a few weeks of this, they realized they sounded just like straight parents, and they should leave me be and let me figure it out myself.

It wasn't something they did, or Smith. It wasn't a phase. I'm now married to a woman. We've been together for twenty years, and have three kids. She is my light and my rock, the base from which I build my life.

Our kids are growing up in a different world. When my older daughter was in kindergarten, I was in the classroom one day when a boy at her table asked, "Why don't you have a dad? Did he die?"

Before I could even step in, another girl at the table snapped, "Some kids don't have dads. That's just the way it is and it doesn't matter at all."

It's not always easy for them. They have to explain, in new classrooms, about their parents. Because I grew up with lesbian moms, I think I have some perspective to help them sort out issues, but I know my ability to protect them is limited. I can't tell them how to address questions, and I can't insulate them from homophobia. They have to find their way, as I did. But they have us, as well as a lot of grandmas and aunties and uncles, to walk with them along the way. And I know they'll be just fine.

Recently, my daughter had to deliver a speech for a school assignment. She chose to discuss LGBTQ+ equality. And so I found myself, once again, in a school cafeteria, with the familiar cinderblock walls, the American flag prominently displayed. Fifth graders in brightly colored sneakers and shorts wiggled in the seats around me, and their parents, in more somber colors, gripped various recording devices.

When it was her turn, my beautiful girl, tall and thin with long blonde hair and wide, clear blue eyes, ascended the stage. The screen behind her showed a rainbow flag flapping in the sun. She began, "I have two moms."

With much more grace and bravery than I ever could have mustered at that age, she discussed equality, homophobia, and how far we've come. She ended, the applause echoing through that cavernous cafeteria, with a black and white photo of Susan and me dancing at our wedding.

Susan and I got married in San Francisco on a bright, clear January day. We both wore white, Susan a long coat with a faux fur collar, and I was in a sleek backless gown and an up-do. The chapel was filled with our friends and family—my parents and brother; my grandfather, aunt, and uncle from Janice's side; Susan's neighbors from childhood; my best friend from elementary school; and friends from college, law school, and our jobs as lawyers. Mom and Janice had split up by then, and Mom's new partner, Nancy, was there with her. Nancy has a rich and smooth alto, and she sang for us as we left the chapel, holding hands. She belted out Etta James's "At Last," so loud the stained glass windows shook. Susan pulled me to her in front of the church, and we danced in the late afternoon sun. Our friends and family poured out after us. They surrounded us, talking, laughing, and taking pictures, and in the center of it all, Susan and I danced.

THE FAMILY THAT JUST HAPPENED

OLIVIA RUDIS, age 18

MY PARENTS FOUGHT through my entire childhood, and deep down I knew they wouldn't be together forever. They permanently split in 2009—I was nine, and it was the best/worst day in my memory. As the daddy's girl I am, I took his side. I wasn't necessarily *mad* at my mom, but I didn't cling to her like I did my father. I was fortunate my parents had zero quarrels about custody—my brother and I have spent equal time between them since their divorce.

My mom has always battled depression and worn her heart on her sleeve. Stating that she is an emotional person would be an extreme understatement. My dad is different—a stone, almost Spartan. I can rarely tell what he is *actually* feeling. Ironically, he's also the most honest person you'll ever meet; he says what he thinks and lives his life openly. He excels at pissing people off (which I secretly admire).

My mother moved out of the house, and afterwards we had a period where my dad, brother, and I ate out practically every night. We slept in his bed and watched

TV until sunrise. I thought my dad was literally the coolest because he had, and has, an awesome sense of humor and makes me laugh nonstop.

All that being said, I didn't recognize that he was miserable. He was also depressed my entire childhood prior to my parents' separation. I didn't realize it right away but something was wrong with my dad. As time passed, things started to get slightly better, but I couldn't figure out why.

He started hanging out with his friend Simon very frequently. Simon was the ex-husband of my mom's best friend at the time. I started to mentally question if he was dating Simon. Now that I reflect back, I didn't think twice that I thought my dad was dating a man. I was just suspicious that he wasn't telling me who he was dating. Anyway, none of that was true, as Simon is, like, the straightest, most hetero cisgendered man that exists. He was just being a good friend to my dad by being there for him.

I STARTED NOTICING pictures of my dad and another man around the house. A photo booth picture above the computer, a framed one of them in the office area. It was a gradual imposition that I observed with open eyes. The house became cleaner. We started sleeping in our own rooms. Dad made us dinner and was spending more time with us—he was changing in positive ways.

Thomas, my dad, came out to me in a Bertucci's when I was eleven, and it was the first time I really saw his inner strength and vulnerability. I wasn't mad, upset, or even shocked. I was mostly sad. Sad that my dad was living in secrecy for so long because he couldn't be who he was. People get disappointed when I tell them my dad's lackluster coming out story. Some go, "That's it?" It's not anything dramatic, but it's a special memory I have with him that I will cherish forever.

What *did* shock me was finding out the age of that guy in the pictures gradually filling my house. His name was Brian, and at the time, he was 21 and my dad was 43—more than double his age. Fairly soon after my dad came out, Brian moved in.

I can't remember when I actually met Brian. The first time I saw him was on accident—he barely said a word and walked right past me into the kitchen. I do remember thinking that he was rude. Little did I know he was my dad's boyfriend. Eventually, I thought he was the coolest person on the planet. He was living in a warehouse-turned-apartment in Philly with ten to fifteen other people, was in a band, and covered in tattoos. Brian accepted us right away. I honestly didn't want to accept him, but I couldn't help it—he was and still is the nicest, best, most amazing person ever.

Prior to explaining it to other people, I really didn't think much about the fact that my dad is gay. However, my mom thought about it a lot and made it clear to us that she thought about it a lot. I wouldn't call my mom homophobic then, and I wouldn't now, but she was working through a lot of feelings. She is a kind, loving, and open person who never once made me think being gay or bi or whatever you are is wrong. However, she was very suspicious of Brian, especially because of how young he was. She was clearly having a difficult time processing everything.

Now, I can empathize better with what she was going

through. I still struggle with the feelings I felt towards her when I was younger, but I have a different perspective. I really don't think that my mom hates that my dad is gay. It has to be hard to be married to someone, have children, and then find out they were never attracted to you in that way.

THE FIRST TIME I really felt uncomfortable about someone talking about LGBTQ+ people was in fifth grade. In my class one day, kids were calling each other "gay" or "lesbian." Boys were supposed to be called "lesbians" because they like girls, and girls were supposed to be called "gay" because they like boys. If you disagreed with this game, you were called gross and weird. I quietly held in my anger because the uses of the words were all wrong. Then I was talking to a boy who called me gay, and I responded with, "And you're a lesbian."

"Right," he said.

I went home mad at myself. I knew it wasn't right, but I still conformed to what I was told to do. That night I developed a backbone and decided I wasn't going to be an asshole. Next time I heard someone say "faggot," I was determined to say something. I didn't care if that made some of my classmates think I was stuck-up as much I cared about not hearing that word be used.

When I started to tell people that my dad was gay, I was asked things like, "So does that mean you're gay?" or "Isn't he bi?" or "Why did he lie to you for so long?" Some people said, "He doesn't seem gay." Those are just a few examples. I got particularly upset when other people took it upon themselves to decide what sexual orientation he was. If someone comes out as something, it's none of your business to say you think that they are something else. You're not them, you're only you.

In the gay community, my dad is considered a "bear." I'm not sure what the gay term for my stepdad is, as he is unique. Frequently, people want to see a picture of my dad. I know what they are expecting—a flamboyant stereotype. Much to their surprise, my dad is covered in hair, large and in charge, wears cargo shorts year-round, and snarky T-shirts. "Oh, he doesn't look gay!" is the usual response. When they meet him, "He doesn't sound gay!" is another popular one. On occasion, people will debate whether or not he is *actually* gay. It truly is a mystery to me how a person thinks it's acceptable to argue that because someone doesn't have the 'look' it means they're not gay.

MY DAD WAS diagnosed with leukemia in 2011. It happened shortly after Brian moved in. That was the scariest time ever for our family, but Brian held us together. No one in our family could deny that he is the reason we didn't fall into a million pieces. He took care of my brother and me, my mom, my extended family, and was the best partner to my dad. Brian took us to and from school, packed our lunches, made us dinner, and made us think everything was going to be all right. With all of that weight on his shoulders, he still was cautious to never show he was scared in front of us. He was and is the strongest person I know. He's my hero. I didn't find out until more recently that my dad told Brian if he wanted to leave, he would understand. But Brian stayed. He showed us that he loved us and proved he wanted to be a part of our lives as a father. Brian is our father.

After that period of my life, I became angrier with people who made comments about my family. I didn't tell my dads about the things people said—I still don't tell them, I'm not sure why. Maybe it's because I don't want them to be hurt, or wonder if it hurts me. I became enraged, because how could someone question if my family was legitimate? Because it wasn't traditional or what The Bible said was right? I got sick of making excuses for people. That they just didn't know, or they hadn't grown up with an open family, or they were old or old-fashioned. All of those things are bullshit. They are no longer excuses, and never should have been in the first place.

For three years in high school I went to an all-girl private Catholic school. Why I thought that was a good idea is beyond me. It sucked. But I had a few amazing teachers and met my two best friends there. My junior year English teacher was the best teacher I had ever had in my life. Both my deans were amazing, and one was even a nun. I had a few incidents with teachers who made comments about my family. I would report it and nothing would really be done, because teachers can get away with anything in a Catholic school.

Because it was a Catholic school, homophobia was common and accepted. My all-girl school had dances, and girls couldn't go with each other, even as friends. I didn't like how most people's defense of their ignorance towards the LGBTQ+ community was, "Well in the Bible . . ." or "God . . ." I am not personally religious, but I do believe in freedom of religion. I also think that something that calls someone to act violently or oppress others is not religion. If there is a God, He would not give a shit about who you love or how you want to identify. There would be far more important things on His plate.

But my school was also considered one of the more progressive ones. Most of my peers were great and open-minded people. Sometimes, after explaining my family situation someone would say "Oh, my uncle's gay" or "My cousin's neighbor's daughter is a lesbian" to validate to themselves and show me that they weren't homophobic.

My dads rarely display affection in public. When I was younger I asked my dad why, and he told me it's because they do not want anybody saying anything negative to them. This was early on in their relation-ship, and I'm not sure if that reason remains. We haven't talked about it since. Honestly, Brian and my dad aren't really the PDA type, but the fact that my dad told me the reason they don't is frustrating. I don't know if anyone has ever said anything negative to my dad and Brian, because they've never told me. I don't think anyone has, but I've never asked. Frankly, I don't want to.

Throughout my childhood, I had never seen so much judgment and hatred towards my family and families like mine than recently. I've met so many open-minded people as well, but hate resonates with you more. Family members who have known for years about my dad are now saying negative things about his sexual orientation. Friends and co-workers say things as well. Why now? Because they feel invited to do so. It's terrifying.

I'm so scared of people. I'm not just worried about someone saying something mean to my dad or Brian, I'm scared of someone hurting them. We hear far too often that someone is beaten or killed for being gay, or being black, or wearing a hijab. It's frustrating that I have that fear in the back of my head.

Looking at my life, I feel so thankful. I'm thankful for all the love I have and the privileges. I'm thankful for all the perspectives I have. I actually feel prouder of my family now. I'm proud that my family isn't traditional. I wouldn't change a thing.

THROUGH RAINBOW-COLORED GLASSES

ERIC TRACY-COHEN, age 26

I COME FROM a very diverse and open LGBTQ+ household—I have five mothers and no real father figure. When it comes to raising and or having a child, a lesbian couple has fairly limited options. My parents arranged for an open adoption with my birthmother, Janet. From my understanding, they spent a lot of time getting acquainted with her beforehand. Additionally, they promised to stay in touch and keep her in my life once I was adopted, which I'm beyond grateful for.

Personally, I think that being in contact with the woman who didn't *want* to give me up but had no other option opened my eyes later in life. As a child, I didn't understand the circumstances very well—I never had any animosity towards her, but I didn't have the knowledge to comprehend the full situation. I saw her about once a year, and I believe had I not been raised in this inclusive way, I would have turned out very differently than I did.

The best thing that could have happened to me was being able to know everything about my family history and where I came from. I still see Janet on occasion, and have a great relationship with her extended family as well. I have a half-brother named Jamie who lives with her, and my cousins Prince, Franklin, and Charlyn who were adopted into the family, whom I consider siblings as well.

On the flip side, I know several other adopted kids from LGBTQ+ families and otherwise—most of whom did not have the option of meeting or knowing their birthparents. Either their adoptive families chose not to tell them who they were, or their birth families actively sought to block them from their lives. My opinion is that this can be destructive to those kids. For children who have judgment and bigotry thrown at them solely based on their parents' situation, it can be extremely traumatizing. From my experience, knowing your background is crucial for the healthy development of a child as both an individual and a person.

The takeaway from being in an open adoption to an LGBTQ+ family is knowing that your birth family is not judging your adoptive family because of who they are. When I speak to my birthmother, it's obvious that she didn't care what my family comprised—all she wanted was assurance that her child would be raised in a loving home.

While growing up in an LGBTQ+ family was great, we still had our ups and downs, just like any other "normal" family.

My brother was adopted from a different family, but unfortunately had the exact opposite circumstances as me. Originally, his was an open adoption, but then his birthmother decided she didn't want to have a connection and ended up cutting off all contact with him. In school, he became a very popular athlete—star quarterback and so on. However, I always felt my brother was struggling internally with our family situation. Due to peer pressure, he kept trying to fit in and I think he may have been ashamed of our out-and-open family before distancing himself and turning to his friends and drugs.

I'm three years older than him, but I was more of a theater geek and he was a jock. He bullied me often, hitting me and causing fights or incidents that he successfully blamed on me. These altercations caused a rift between us that has never completely healed. I feel that some of his actions may have root at the fact that I had the constant connection to my birth family and he did not.

As a child, when things in my life derailed, reading was my escape. I dove into fantastical worlds of fables and fiction. I was attracted to the characters who were plagued by troubles or a lack of acceptance, and it caused them to head out on their own. Books like that really spoke to me and helped inspire what I've done, which is step out of my comfort zone and talk about my family. Some of the biggest influences in my childhood aside from family members were authors, many of whom I've been lucky enough to meet, some of whom I hope I will get to meet in the near future.

Alongside reading, one of my biggest escapes was anime. First, because I loved the art and effort—diligence that went into creating true step-by-step animated work. I'm referring to authentic Japanese animation. It's a blast to watch, but the true reason I enjoy it is because of the fan community attached to it.

I became acquainted with the anime community and comic conventions during freshman year of college. I was drawn to cosplay and costuming because of my interest in making and building unusual things. My first cosplay was Howl from the movie *Howl's Moving Castle*. I was nervous, but my introductory convention was one of the most inclusive events I'd ever experienced. I felt safe, and discovered that everyone had the same interest in anime that I had. This was a game-changing experience for me.

Overall, the attendees and cosplayers were some of the nicest and friendliest people I'd met in a long time. I was not judged, and no one seemed to care what my sexual orientation was. I discovered there are a lot of LGBTQ+ cosplayers and they often converge at these conventions. I love to invite my LGBTQ+ friends who are into anime, and when they go to these conventions they can just be themselves. My takeaway is that you can be who and whatever you want to be, even if it's just for one or two days. You can use a costume, headpiece, or anything you want to express yourself, and you don't have to worry about anyone judging you. We all belong to the same community.

WHEN I STARTED school, I was teased quite often, and frequently asked why I didn't have a dad, or where my dad was, or why I had so many parents. I quickly surmised that the more open I was about my situation, my family, and my personal views on life, the less I was teased and the more people started to accept me for who I was. Something everyone should consider is that the best way to be accepted is just to be open and honest about *everything*. It can be very uncomfortable, and I wish that wasn't the case, but I've found the ideal way to facilitate dialogue is just by talking about yourself.

Regardless of my beliefs, I had a very *Spy vs. Spy* relationship with *one* kid throughout my entire educational experience. He and I go way back, and honestly I'm not really sure how it started. Something unknown happened in middle school, and every time we saw each other, we got in fights because he would make fun of my hair or my mother's. I retaliated with insults or fists. It seemed that every week we found new ways to ambush each other. It became absolutely exhausting.

Years passed, and we didn't reunite until I was a sophomore in high school, where we serendipitously ended up in biology class together. We were neutral for several weeks until one thing led to another—we got into an awful fight, resulting in my detention and his suspension. From what I could gather, he ended up transferring out of school shortly after that. I regarded that as a total win against a bully who deserved it.

Believe it or not, the saga continued into college, when I was studying film at De Anza. Ironically, he began to attend the same school as I did. I randomly saw him in the cafeteria and was shocked. I puffed up my chest and walked over, calling him out by name. When he recognized me, I could tell he thought I would initiate a fight. However, diplomacy settled in and we hugged and made up. I have never seen him since, but I'm happy that we both had the chance to reconcile our differences. That moment proved to me that people *can* change. I'm still not sure how we made up like we did, but it's clear that we both grew somewhere along the way.

It is experiences like these that can change peoples' lives. While I categorize these "incidents" as small, they had a profound impact on the direction of my life. School became my safe space where I joined backstage production, building the sets and props for our shows. I didn't realize it at the time, but this decision concurrently saved my life and built the foundation for my profession. I am now a production designer and independent film producer. My work is focused on promoting diversity and changing perceptions. At this point in my life, I rarely have problems and I think I get along fairly well even with people who have different viewpoints about life and sexuality.

The second I became open about my life, personal beliefs, and family is the second I was teased less and treated more fairly. People are scared of the unknown. Once you educate them, that fear diminishes. This realization made my path of acceptance clearer, and eventually I made many quality friends. The additional benefit of being raised in an LGBTQ+ family is that kids are curious—and when you satisfy their curiosity openly without evasion, they're generally like, "Oh . . . cool." This technique affected my life in positive ways once I graduated high school. In college, I pursued my dream of working in film. Now, I'm able to gear my work towards promoting a more diverse world in the industry and trying to touch on points that other people are afraid to.

OUR PARENTS DIVORCED when I was going into middle school, which in hindsight threw an interesting twist into an already unorthodox household. The situation stabilized slightly, a couple years after they each found partners. It was a rocky start, and being a child, I didn't get along well with my new stepmothers. Going into high school, I finally found a balance and accepted they were happy. I began making a bigger effort to get along with my recently added family members.

I think it was beneficial for me to have four or five mothers just for the fact that I'm not a typical guy. I'm more in tune with my feminine side, which I'm open about. I am able to get along famously with women. Sometimes I wish I had a father figure, but I observe my friends who are typical frat boy types and realize that's not really me. I'm thankful for my family; because of the fact that they are transparent helped me keep an open mind.

The San Francisco Bay Area is known for being accepting of almost everything, but it saddens me that where I grew up in Palo Alto there was still some stereotyping and hatred towards the LGBTQ+ community. While unfortunately there remain those people who cause problems, the benefit to having family that is out and proud is their willingness to support you with anything. They were there to explain the problems that I was facing. They were willing to talk to me about what I might face in growing up.

A perk of being raised in a family like mine is that I am more open-minded than most. If you want to get into the sociology, I guess I would be considered pansexual if you *had* to label me. But it's really more than that—I don't care what my partner looks like or their gender. I care more about the person underneath, the person that I'm spending time with. Their personality, interest level, and commonalities are what I regard as important. I won't judge you based on what you look like or your sexual orientation.

Some people try to judge, harass, or tease me. But I know who I am and I don't particularly care what anyone else thinks of me. People seem to notice this, and I tend to attract the ones that are open to debate. Due to my openness, I have many dear friends that were raised with different faiths and cultural outlooks on life.

I will freely admit the harassment can still bug me sometimes, but I'm successful and happy enough with myself that I just avoid the people that treat me poorly.

Due to my willingness to talk about my family and myself, I have met a lot of people that share my views on life, and also a lot that don't. I believe the best industry for LGBTQ+ youth and family is entertainment. Behind the scenes, most of the stage crew care more about what you can do than what your background is. Ironically there are several actors that I work with who may be some of the most conservative people I know. I had no clue about this until I friended them on social media—I was quite shocked. I had known them professionally for about a year beforehand and they had no issues being around me. But this is a perfect example of how you can still be friends with those individuals that have different views, as long as you're open to hearing differing opinions.

One of the gentlemen of whom I speak, I call on quite frequently for gigs, and his views never come up in conversation. He respects my family and still asks about my former partner. I feel that while he had a different upbringing, he respects me as a producer and a person and therefore he does not judge me for my life choices.

TO OVERCOME ADVERSITY and pain, you must be willing to accept that these things exist. You don't need to change yourself, you just need to be *true* to yourself, and willing to put that foot forward. Sometimes you may face rejection, but most often people will be tolerant and your true friends will choose to be with you. I've been lucky that most people I've met have been very accepting. Unfortunately, I know people that weren't accepted by their families, and who weren't proud to talk about their families. I think that is possibly one of the biggest issues facing our community.

People can be scared to talk about themselves, or if they do, it will be with a chosen few. I believe the ideal way to live in the LGBTQ+ community, even if you have fears of rejection, is to talk about it with someone. Be willing to put it out there, which is exactly what I'm trying to do with my work. I am a very creative person and am fortunate enough to be successfully making a living in the industry of my choosing. It is important for me to reach out through film to the people in our community who are feeling disrespected and provide them that opportunity to feel comfortable talking about themselves. Also, I want to give them someone they can relate to.

In my attempts to bring out more diversity in film, I have met some fascinating people – famous or other-wise – and they've been very encouraging. The second I became very involved and open about my life, opportunities just blossomed. Yes, I've been rejected; yes, I've been treated badly; but overall, it's been a positive experience. No matter where I go and whom I talk to, there is always someone there who will support me. I credit that pride to my upbringing and my LGBTQ+ family.

I've had many peaks and valleys in my life— throughout my childhood, teen years, and now. I frequently discuss my successes in overcoming challenges to any willing ears. I like to explain that even if life throws you negativity, eventually it will even out and positivity will return. Life isn't worth living if everything's fucking perfect. Those peaks and valleys are *necessary* to fully enjoy and appreciate it.

I've doubted where I'm at before. I've doubted connections; I've doubted my purpose. The eye-opener for me was when I got my first place to myself and opened that door. That's when I realized that I had made it, and I said out loud, "I am happy, I found my place here, I am home now."

I can attribute most, if not all, of these achievements to the family members and other people who believed in me. When you are working towards a goal, a place, an opportunity, or even to prove yourself, it always appears to be an uphill battle. But, at any moment you can turn around and realize that you can change yourself. When you begin to struggle, remember that you can ask for help from your support network. That network is there for you. You just have to find them. If you don't know how, ask me, and I will help you find them. And I will be the beginning of your support network. By reading my story, you have made one new friend in me.

THE WAY IT WAS FOR ME

KELLEN KAISER, age 36

I WAS BORN at home in 1981, in a place perched in the fog south of San Francisco. Inside the house with low ceilings, cluttered with Native American art and Buddhist religious objects, my petite blonde mom lay naked on a brass bed, breathing like a steam engine, to the encouragements brought forth from the other three ladies. The birth was attended by my mother's lover, my mother's best friend, and a midwife.

"You are the strongest woman we know, you can do this," cheered the best friend, a youthful fifty-five-year-old. She looked at the midwife for approval.

The midwife brought in for the occasion told the birthing woman, "You're doing good, not much longer, keep pushing," as the other two women sat beside the bed. Together they were trying to rephrase the nuclear family as something re-envisioned, reborn as triumvirate. The labor lasted through the night, and into the morning.

As fate would have it, I got stuck, my clavicles unable to dislodge from my mother's hips. The group fretted. If they had been in a hospital, standard procedure might have forced them to break the baby's bones.

"But we will try to do it the old-fashioned way. The way you'd help a cow," the midwife said.

My biological mother is a little woman. Despite her possession of an outsize personality, she is barely five feet tall, though she'd never admit to it, and hadn't weighed over one hundred pounds before getting pregnant. I weighed almost nine pounds at the outset, so it was a bad combination. The midwife had to cut an inch of skin to reach in and turn me and pull me out blue. She christened me by blowing air into my little mouth, telling my gathered mothers she was giving me my first kiss. That was how I came into the world—covered in the kisses of women.

The community that I was raised in was distinctly "womyn-centered": womyn's bookstores, womyn's healthcare cooperatives, and womyn's newspapers, like the one in which my mother's best friend advertised the opportunity to come camp at her ranch in exchange for working the land. A chance that led to her and my mother meeting and together co-producing a womyn's music festival, one in which hundreds of womyn, many bare-breasted, cavorted in a womyn-only space. When, for some reason, necessity required men showing up, "Man on the Land" was shouted out to give ladies enough time to get their shirts back on.

In my mother's house, we had a women's sign on our bathroom door. We had so few men visit that it wasn't a problem until 1991, when my brother was born. In my family, we went to "Take Back the Night" rallies, colored pictures of diverse vulvas, and played a card game called, "Great Women," in which you traded mighty foremothers like Elizabeth Cady Stanton for Sojourner Truth to make pairs, a bit like rummy. At some point each member of my family sported a mullet. We were iconically queer.

My first name, Kellen, came from a therapist. She was counseling my mother and her lover at the time, my godmother. Theirs was a relationship not meant to be, and the therapist perhaps was aware, telling them to work on something easy, say, a baby name. One advocated Kelly, but the other, aghast, proclaimed that "No Kelly would be in the White House" and offered Virginia or Helen, more dignified or precedented options. The therapist by then was probably sure that they were doomed but gave them the name—Kellen—which she explained meant "amazon" in Gaelic. What more could they want? We're talking early 80s lesbians, here.

Growing up in San Francisco meant I lived in the closest thing to a gay Mecca there was in the States, and my parents did everything in their power to make the place even more progressive. My parents raised me in an intentional and devoted manner. They were both protective and very courageous. They founded the first LGBTQ+ parents' association, held in-services for my teachers, and lobbied to get books featuring families like ours into my school libraries. They got school forms changed to say "parent," instead of "mother and father."

Still, when I was growing up, all the years were Reagan years for quite a while, the first seven in a row and from where I lived, in the most liberal pocket of America, this meant we had a constant source of complaint at hand. We protested his foreign policy in Latin America, his stance on nuclear weapons, his refusal to talk about the plague in our community (or really, our community at all). As an elementary-school-aged child, I participated in the resistance by collecting pennies for pencils in Nicaragua, holding signs with crossed-out warheads, and bringing meals to folks who were dying of AIDS.

My mom worked as a homecare/hospice nurse, so despite the insular nature of the womyn's community at that point, the epidemic destroying our city loomed large in my childhood. Funerals were far too common. In one particularly poignant moment from 1987, I gifted a few of my favorite teddy bears to a young man, who in drag pulled off an awesome Ann Margaret, only to receive them back a few months later, post-funeral. Part of being the daughter of lesbians meant being adult before my time.

It was common when I was growing up for people to exclaim that they'd never met anyone with gay parents before, upon meeting me. For a long time, I earnestly believed that I was the first kid ever with lesbian moms, because I'd never met anyone older who could claim the title. My admission of my parents' queerness was regularly followed with a request for me to explain my family structure to that person's satisfaction, followed by the inevitable question, "but which one is your real mom?" That is probably my least favorite question of all time.

By the time I hit puberty I had debated countless adults defending both my parents' sexuality and their right to raise me as they saw fit. People would comment on how mature and articulate I was, unaware that my preciousness related to confronting adult issues before my time—folks inquiring as to my sexuality before it had a chance to develop and of course, being asked about my parents' sex life. Gay parents were considered deviant, and so I spent a lot of my childhood on the defensive, insisting that we were like everyone else, even when I knew there were lots of ways we were different.

I had more moms than anyone else I knew. The original three were joined by a fourth who married my mother in a non-legally binding wedding when I was five, years after her relationship with my godmother dissolved. In my mother's life, the rule seemed to follow that when romantic relationships fail, the folks become family. A family that expanded when I was ten with the arrival of my younger sibling. With the added space my brother took up, the house I grew up in felt even smaller, with three adults, two kids, five cats and three dogs all cramped together in a two-bedroom house, and so we moved across the Bay in search of higher square footage for our dollar.

We were typical enough to move to the suburbs. El Sobrante, where we ended up, is an unincorporated area next to the large, industrial city of Richmond that had its heyday in the ship building years of World War II. El Sobrante, which means "the leftovers," is a rural sliver in its shadow. We moved there because it was one of the last vaguely affordable spots in the Bay Area.

The fact that it was unincorporated meant that there was no local government, no police force outside of the county sheriff, and no city taxes. This led to a very diverse population. There were bikers and meth-makers evading the law, there were militia members avoiding taxes and government, and loads of working people and immigrants enjoying the affordability. There were also families who had been living there since before it was developed and had stayed. From where we lived on the crook of a turn in the road, I could see some person's horse from my backyard. Once we moved in, there was also one gay family, at least.

The house we moved into was bigger by two bedrooms and had a sizeable backyard for the pets. Our neighbor was a lady who watched the world from her front window with the aid of binoculars. She assured us we would never get robbed, not with her around. This seemed like the kind of place where people knew each other. Maybe I could get to know the kids in the area and run around more. We were in a vaguely suburban neighborhood that could have translated into increased freedom of movement for me. In the city, the crackhouse that sat between my best friend's house and mine had prevented us from walking to and fro.

"The suburbs are where the really bad things happen, though," said my mom. "I'm sure this place is full of child molesters."

"Well, let me investigate that with the kids around here," I offered. "I'll find out."

"That's what I'm afraid of," she said, as I raced out the door.

I spent the afternoon roaming a five-block radius with a collection of children whom I had come upon a street over from my house. Of that gaggle, the most interesting to me was a blond kid with a shaved head and bright blue eyes; my earliest prototype of "handsome." Alas, he wanted to introduce me to Jesus.

"I go to El Sobrante Christian Day School," he said. *Our love will be a forbidden one*, I thought. "Have you accepted Christ as your personal savior?" he said with a smile tinted blue from the powdered candy he'd been eating.

"Um, no. I'm Jewish, actually," I replied. This usually ended the conversation.

"Huh. Well, you can still come to Christ, I think. You might just have to repent or something."

At his house, I was offered a turkey sandwich but had to refuse it, on account of being a vegetarian. The blond boy looked at me, confused.

"You wanna head back to your place? I have to ride my bike over to Bible camp. You can come though, if you want."

No, I'd already been gone longer than I should have. I looked around the dim living room lit by the TV. All the kids looked like the scrappy heroes in a movie like *The Goonies*. At home when I told my moms about the kids and their love of Bible camp, they did not encourage more interaction.

A house a couple of doors down from us proudly displayed the yellow "don't tread on me" flag with its coiled snake. A block over, a garage sale revealed on one wall of the opened garage a massive swastika flag. It was being used as a backdrop for a motorcycle that was being sold. The whole scene made me nervous.

I had a bit of a persecution complex as a child. Blame should partially rest on my mother exposing me at a very early age to the worst consequences of injustice.

I have singed into my memory a picture of a body in a charred car, the victim of a lynching, thanks to an unsanctioned viewing of a video sent to my mom by an anti-racism organization to which she donated. My parents were unabashed in explaining oppression to me. I used the terms racism, anti-semitism, and homophobia with ease in elementary school. On the other hand, my awareness led to my demanding we take down the straw Star of David that hung on our front door during the holiday season. What if neo-Nazis came and found us because of it?

"Well, we have an attack-cat sticker displayed on our door, that should scare them off," said my mother. She brushed her hand over my hair, pulled me closer to her.

"I'm serious," I whined.

But persecution-wise, I'd personally have a lot more to worry about at my new middle school. America's oldest secular girls school on the west coast; I was sent there because my mothers had a complete faith in single-sex education. They'd agreed that my confidence would be best maintained in a classroom full of other girls. I wouldn't dumb myself down in order to impress the boys. I would be judged on my brain, not my body. After all, my godmother had attended Wellesley and her mother had attended Vassar and it had worked out well for them.

I had applied in the fifth grade, but my math wasn't up to par. That's the kind of school it was, a fifth grader could be sufficiently behind so as not to be accepted. After two years of tutoring it was decided I could keep up and was accepted. There, the theory held, I would grow into a smart and confident young woman who was used to speaking her mind in front of her peers. It was supposed to be a sympathetic audience for my intellect.

There were some early and strong signs that this wouldn't go well for me. We'd been invited as one of the new families entering the school to attend a "New Families Tea." I'm not sure what my parents thought this would consist of. We had all drunk tea in the past, I'd forced tea parties on them that had included teddy bears, and yet we should have done some further research before heading over there.

The school itself was housed in a gigantic mansion propped up on a hill in ritzy Pacific Heights, and it poured down the knoll into a more modern building. The whole place oozed old money and power. Up to the heavy front doors of the mansion/school we trotted. My mom was in jeans and a T-shirt. I was wearing leggings and a sweatshirt. My brother was only wearing a onesie over his diaper and some shorts. We took a deep breath and heaved open one side of the giant doors.

Inside it was darker, but we glanced in just long enough to reveal a man in tails sitting at a grand piano as a father-daughter couple swirled gracefully by, doing a dance I'd only seen in movies. He was in a suit and she was in a floor-length gown. We shut the door to that strange other universe and all in agreement, having not said a thing, we all went home.

The first day of school, I was hoping no one would bring it up. Chubby, with two French braids in my hair and a slip under my uniform, I arrived.

"Did you go to the New Families Tea?" one impossibly thin and well put-together young girl asked. It hadn't been an hour, it was still first period.

"No, I didn't go. I don't even know what one of those things is, you know?"

Every class brought new humiliation. During gym, I discovered that the key to dealing with the transparent quality of my deeply unflattering sailor's middy and pleated, knee-length skirt lay in wearing a gym uniform underneath it. No one had mentioned any such thing to us at the uniform shop. My moms and I had gone over a few different options for modesty's sake before going with the slip. Now I couldn't participate and I was sure a few girls snickered when I explained why I couldn't strip down. That day I cursed my mother and the antique undergarments she'd put me in.

While not having alerted me to the need for gym clothes, the uniform shop had however managed to hoist seven pairs of knee socks upon me, which by lunch I'd learned were not *de riguer*. I was told that by a girl in the grade above me, who "helped" me roll them down in a way that was vaguely socially acceptable. If I couldn't replace them… I could already hear my mom's response.

"I'm not buying you another fourteen socks, that's ridiculous," my mother would say. There was no point in asking. But upon correcting the height of the socks, another horrific discovery had been made. I didn't shave my legs. I was a "sasquatch" in their terms—what, had I been raised by lesbians? At home that night I begged my moms to allow me some sort of hair removal.

"You're too young for that sort of thing," a mom intoned.

"Shaving is just a patriarchal way of keeping women looking prepubescent. You should be proud that you are growing into a beautiful young woman," said another mom with hairy legs of her own.

"I don't want you to slip and scrape part of your leg off."

I told them I would rather die before returning to that school with hairy legs. A bottle of Nair was bought and my only experience with that product ensued. Maybe they realized that I would have far greater battles than leg hair ahead of me at that school.

A week into the school year, my whole seventh grade class took a trip to Yosemite National Park. The school ran K-8, meaning that most of my class had known each other as long as they could remember. The trip was supposed to integrate the three new girls, including myself, into the existing social structure. The beauty of the surrounding landscape left no impression upon me. Instead I remember only three things from that trip: getting stung by bees, learning to shower with my bathing suit on, and sealing my fate as unpopular.

There were so many unsaid social codes that I wasn't privy to. Where had all these girls learned them? Was this the difference between having gay parents and straight ones? Did straight parents know all these rules by heart and pass them on unconsciously?

I made my first friend by breaking one of the thousands of rules I didn't know. I showered and walked out of the stall naked to grab my towel. A well-meaning classmate revealed to me my faux pas and came to my rescue.

"What are you doing? You're naked!"

Yeah, I thought, *that's how you shower, right? In the nude.*

"Look, you have two options. You can either shower with your bathing suit on or keep your towel in the stall or nearby enough so that you can put it on before you walk out. Otherwise people will think you're a freak."

I was thankful she was keeping me from that fate. From then on, I only showered with a bathing suit on, if any other girls were in the vicinity. Only in middle school was I taught by my peers that the body should be covered up. It was the antithesis of the way I'd been reared. Confined by clothing during the school day, I would welcome myself home by disrobing, a sort of relaxation. The middle-school modesty bled, for a short while, into my home life, but it was hard to keep up.

The bees came about when we had been separated into pairs to "get to know each other." I'm not sure what the pairs comprised of people who'd known each other since kindergarten had to say to each other, but my buddy and I sat down on a log to chat. A yellow jacket flew over and sat itself on my hand. I had been told that in this situation the right response was just to keep perfectly still and it would fly away. I felt particularly betrayed then when it stung me. I burst into the air with a howl and leaped away from my perch on the log.

From the ether around me, bees burst onto the scene. The log had held their hive. I brushed them out of my hair, down my exposed calves as they stung me all over. I ran as I tried to shake them off my body. If there had been a body of water around I surely would have jumped in it. I wanted immediately to go home and be comforted by my assortment of mothers.

Instead, once I had managed to elude my insect pursuers and remove those riding on me, I was covered with calamine lotion by a nonplussed teacher. She then told me to rejoin the group lest I miss any of the programming, which was mostly for my benefit, since I was one of the new girls. I whimpered my way through the rest of the "bonding activities." I spent the evening counting the twenty-seven stings, which were already swollen and itchy, and upon assessing the situation, felt a large amount of self-pity, which I then continued to wallow in for the next two years.

The only break from my doldrums that year was the time I got pulled out of math class to go talk on CNN. It was 1993 and a lesbian woman named Sharon Bottoms had lost custody of her two-year-old son in the Virginia courts. The international news station wanted an expert opinion to weigh in. Thanks to being in possession of lesbian parents and a winning person-ality, I had been called upon to defend my people in the national spotlight.

Clad in my school-girl uniform, I attested to the fact that my family was as good as everyone else's. We ate dinner together, they helped me with my homework. I gave testimony to the "normalcy" of my family in order to assure the American public that families like mine had the right to exist. It may be presumptuous asking someone to reflect on their family, in that way, at such a young age, but it was necessary. In the media, preachers warned about the "gay agenda" and suggested that homosexuals were child molesters. Pat Robertson, Jerry Fallwell and James Dobson "focused on the family" by trying to malign mine.

Being a media spokesperson meant that even when I was at my most angsty and alienated as a teen, I knew that I had to put on a show for the world at large. Arguments between my parents and me were postponed long enough for the cameras to do their job. It was an odd sort of fishbowl. On one hand, it was pretty exciting to be yanked out of class to talk on TV and I thought I could milk it for popularity. On the other hand, it was because my family's rights were under attack. Being special can have its downsides.

Growing up as the daughter of four lesbians, there are things I have always known. For me there is no time before them. I don't remember a time when I didn't know my parents were lesbians. I don't remember a time when I didn't know what that word means. I don't remember the first time I talked to the media, maybe because I've been explaining my family for longer than my memory stretches back. I am an ever-evolving teachable moment for the rest of the world to study.

For myself, I am constantly investigating what meaning my parents' sexuality may hold for my life, whether it is in writing my memoir or figuring out how many dates to go on before bringing up my lesbian mothers. My life still serves for me and others as an informal petri dish, a longitudinal survey of what gay parenting's effects may be. And in that way, I am still reflecting on things I don't really have enough perspective yet to speak on. Still hazarding guesses based on a sample size of one.

Although my mother insists she could tell I was straight by the time I was in preschool, my own sexuality has been the source of interest for strangers and friends alike. My personal life regularly juxtaposed against the question, *does having gay parents make you gay?*

As a teenager, my friends who were questioning their sexuality headed instinctually in my direction. Was it because they secretly believed I was a dyke or because I presented as a sort of queer ambassador with a key to the kingdom, even as I dated guy after guy? The effect of my parents' sexuality on my own romantic relationships was of enough interest to me that I decided to write my book exploring that. As more and more photo essays, documentaries, and TV shows like *Modern Family*, *The Fosters* and *The New Normal* represent the experience of queer families, it is important our own voices be included.

Every few years it seems American culture revisits what effect gay parenting has, finds the same answer (the kids are all right), and then repeats the process over again. As each new study confirms that gay parents produce healthy, emotionally stable children, I try to apply my own life into their metric and see that I match up well enough. I have been very lucky to have the family I've been blessed with in this life. My parents are endlessly supportive, we are all very close and they are brilliant individuals who continuously inspire me.

I have a unique perspective at this point, being as old as I am. While nowadays estimates place the number of children with gay parents in the multiple millions, when I was growing up there were a few thousand of us, making me somewhat of a pioneer. I have been watching studies like this come out for a long time. I am now someone who can get away with saying things like, "Back in my day." It's funny to find myself in a place where I feel like a community elder.

There is a certain thrill when I spot my compatriots

out in the world. We are an invisible club with automatic membership. At a roller derby match years back now, I spotted someone I thought might be a fellow daughter of dykes. For those who are not "in the know," roller derby is a sport resurrected from the 1970s, in which women on roller skates beat each other up. Added to this is a level of drama akin to professional wrestling. Miss Evil sporting an eye patch takes down Cecilia B. Demented who sports an ineffective straitjacket. Perhaps because of its embrace of female power and physicality, the sport has a large lesbian membership and following.

This is how I found myself leaning forward in my seat and staring at some sixteen-year-old in the row ahead of me. She was seated between two women who, based on my keen and honed "gaydar," I assumed to be lesbians and possibly her mothers. Trying to listen without being any more obvious than my body language already revealed, I caught one woman speaking to her, and in the tone and content of their exchange it was clear that she was not her mother. But still there was the one left, and the girl didn't seem to be quite old enough to have driven herself there, so maybe she was *queerspawn*.

It didn't make sense really any other way, two older ladies just chatting with some random teenager between them. My heart quickened, I couldn't help myself. I was curious to see whether she was like me, even as I questioned what, if anything, I shared with someone based on their parents' sexuality alone. If I had approached my teenage target, I'm not sure what exactly I would have said, except for a supportive salute. I've never known what to say when people introduce me to other kids with gay parents, because the jury is still out on what we exactly share. A friend introduced me to another girl he knew, saying, "She's got more moms than you do. I didn't believe it was possible." When we sat down awkwardly to compare, it turned out we were equal in amount of moms, and then we were clueless what to say next.

"I got a bunch of moms."

"Yeah, me too."

"Cool . . . So. . . ."

Maybe it's that we don't have the sense of novelty around it that people with straight parents do. For us, it's just our lives.

I am an expert only on myself, and not really that, even. Like any other human, we are just like everyone else and also completely different from anyone else who's ever lived. Maybe I should have offered her my number and told her to call me if she ever needs dating advice.

LEARNING TO LOVE

MARY HOLLAND, age 27

ON OCTOBER 28, 1992, my life changed forever. I was almost three at the time, and had been shuffled from foster home to foster home with my two biological sisters since before I could remember. I don't recall much about those early dwellings now, but I do know that the family home I entered on that date was the most impactful one of my life. For the next two and a half years, I would learn how to love and become part of a functioning family.

On June 12, 1995, I was five-and-a-half when a judge told me that the two women who'd been raising me were now my legal guardians. Their names are Linda and Kathy—though I would only ever call Linda my mom. Kathy always insisted on being called Kathy. For the longest time, I wondered why and even to this day, twenty-two years later, I still am not sure of the reason behind it.

So began my life as the "child of dykes," as the kids in my school would later call it. I grew up in small-town Kansas, smack-dab in the middle of Bible Belt, USA. I knew from an early age I was different, but I didn't know how or why. My family was all I had ever known so I didn't think anything about it was unusual. However, I surmised early on that something was up because I never got invited over to classmates' houses to play. I never made any actual friends at all. The only person I spent time with outside of my sisters was this girl whose mom worked with mine. Her name was Kelsey and she was nice, but we never really stayed that close. As I got older I realized that our only reason for being "friends" was because our moms made it happen.

This led me to having a very lonely childhood. I delved deeply into books and writing. It gave me comfort knowing that in the books that lined my walls, I could escape into worlds where I could be anything I wanted to be. In these worlds, I wasn't lonely, because I was never alone when I had my books. The most precious to me was the *Harry Potter* series. J.K. Rowling created a universe where I felt included, a part of something enormous and majestic. I considered that group of characters my friends, and I could turn to them to find warmth when I desperately needed it. Her words spoke to me more deeply than anyone in my reality ever has. I attribute a lot of who I am now to those books that guided me through my toughest years.

My mom and Kathy tried their best to make me feel worthy and deserving of love. For the most part, I believed them, but there was an underlying problem that persists to this day. Kathy was always cruel in her jokes—especially towards me. I never mentioned this to Mom because I feared her reaction to it would be the same as Kathy's whenever I'd ask her to stop. I feared

Mom would tell me to buck up and stop being so sensitive. Logic told me that my mom would be fair and listen to me, but unfortunately my brain isn't always logical.

As a kid, I endured Kathy telling me to shut up whenever I "talked too much." It shaped who I ended up becoming. I find myself apologizing to my friends today whenever I feel I am talking too much. I always second-guess myself and question whether I'm being annoying. I also find myself holding back at times when I talk to my mom about the things that are really plaguing my heart, because as a child Kathy would frequently tell me to stop bothering my mom with trivial stuff.

I want to believe Mom when she says Kathy loves me, but years of experience have told me otherwise. It was really hard being at home after school and during the summer because my mom worked all day and Kathy stayed home with us. My sisters didn't get as much grief from Kathy because my older sister just ignored it, or didn't let it bother her, and my younger sister was Kathy's favorite. In fact, when I was ten and our family adopted another little girl, I recognized I was the only child in my family who felt like I didn't belong.

That's not to say my life was all bad—not by *any* means!

I fully realize and understand my life is so much better because I was adopted. I never would have become the successful person I am today if it hadn't been for my mom and Kathy. I wouldn't have the big, loud Italian family I have now if it wasn't for them. I wouldn't ever have known love if not for my moms and their extended family.

I just wanted to demonstrate that aspects of my new

life weren't as beautiful and wonderful as most people were led to believe. It wasn't always sunshine and roses (or unicorns and rainbows).

SPENDING ONE-ON-ONE time with my mom was the *best*. In my youth, we discovered that we shared a love for the same movies, which were older 1970s and '80s romance films. As I grew up, we bonded together going to the theater to see all the new romantic comedies, especially if it starred our favorite actress, Meryl Streep.

Additionally, Mom and I both adored books. My passion for reading got her back into her own, mostly because her life was spent working and doing family duties. It was my obsession with *Harry Potter* that compelled her to eventually read the books and later giddily discuss them with me. She also greatly enjoyed when I read books out loud to her as she was working on the computer, or helping my youngest sister with her various needs.

Inevitably, school and books became my favorite places. Not because I had lots of friends, but because I have always loved learning. School was where I *excelled*. I was extremely proficient at language and writing. I started to write when I was in the third grade because I realized that my insecurities were preventing me from speaking about how I felt, but I was comfortable writing about them. I would pour my heart out into a journal that I kept hidden in my room.

When I was about eleven or twelve, my older sister found my journal, to my horror, and exposed all of the feelings I had transcribed. It was devastating.

While I'm well aware that siblings are programmed

to tease—it's kind of their job—my sister was unnaturally adept at picking exactly the perfect second to go for the deepest blow. She masterfully deciphered my most vulnerable moments and then calculated when to strike. One memory I especially abhor came on my twelfth birthday. I received my first-ever portable CD player and I was beyond excited. It was a treasure to me. She, however, took one glance at it and said it looked like "puke." That was the first time I cried on my birthday. To no one's surprise, my sister and I are barely on speaking terms to this day.

It's fair to mention that I struggle with depression, so I sometimes feel the hardest parts of my life are the ones I obsess over. Like I said, I am loved, and I know it. It is because of that love that I can do the things that I do now as an adult.

I was empowered to relocate clear across the country—from Kansas to New York and then later New Jersey—and start my adult life, post-graduation, all on my own. When I first moved, I told myself it was because I needed to figure out how to be truly independent. My mom, always a crutch for me, was the one I had to depend on less. If I was ever in a financial bind, I could rely on her to swoop in and save the day. Granted, it was with a fully detailed repayment plan, but still. She has always been my hero for many reasons.

It was her ability and desire to teach me the strength to be independent that became her paramount life lesson. She taught that while I had her to help me out, I also had to understand what it meant to be financially responsible. To this day, I can budget the hell out of anyone I know because of her.

Over time, I realized the actual reason for transferring to the east coast was that Kansas didn't challenge my thinking or living enough. I needed to be in a place more diverse than farm country, not to diss the Midwest. I needed city life. I needed the realities that come with different communities and groups of people. I think being raised how I was really set me up for a lifetime of saying "yes," or "why not" to many endeavors that others wouldn't know how to handle. My upbringing has given me a sincere compassion for others. My experiences as a child of the LGBTQ+ community have opened my heart to so many people and cultures as I grow and change.

During my youth, I observed how my hometown treated my mom and other gays and it saddened me. I've always worn my hair short because I like not having to worry about hair in general. However, that also meant I was constantly teased by my peers. I learned early on that the words "*dyke*" and "*lesbo*" were derogatory terms. I discovered what it meant to be hurt by words, and how to take those experiences and become stronger for them.

I spent all my formative years without any real friends, but that doesn't mean I was lonely. There were people who'd come and go, based on the fancy of the moment. A few of my classmates "befriended" me when they realized I was a whiz at schoolwork. It was just a ploy to gain my assistance because my desperation to make friends was obvious. They used me for my homework skills and then turned on me when it mattered most. It's a big reason why even to this day I am wary of anyone who wants to be my friend.

My experiences have made me that much more open

to love and all that comes with it. However, I am very sparing in how often I express love because I only seek authentic love. It also means that as an educator I can sense when students are lacking love in their home lives. This causes me to explore different ways to show that I love them. I see their vulnerabilities and I want so badly to help them.

If you were to ask my closest friends, they would tell you my biggest weakness is my insatiable desire to help. I would literally give the shirt off my back if it meant someone less fortunate than me wouldn't be cold. I am known to give away my last dime to others because they need it more than I. That facet of my personality originated from my mom's mom, my nana.

My nana and pop are my all-time favorite people in the world. They are godly individuals who are intrinsically altruistic. They genuinely make me believe that true love exists. Nana and Pop have been in love with each other since they were in their teens, and they are now in their eighties. I know what love is because of them and what they taught their daughter.

I can also identify love because of my mom's sister—she is unabashed in who she loves. Incidentally, it's a woman. Yes, you read that right, my family contains two lesbian couples. My aunt is the one who bestowed upon me strength of character and my wanderlust. She's always encouraged me to never give up on my dreams. In fact, many times she has financed a career-related adventure, just so I wouldn't worry about the expense and could instead focus on becoming a teacher.

While my friends say my weakness is my endless compassion, on the flip it's also my biggest strength. My ability to love and be there for others knows no boundaries. I'm like this not only because of my mom and Kathy, but also because of the rejections I received as a child. There were so many times I wanted friends and a place to belong, only to have negativity thrown back in my face. So now if I ever come across what my mom would call a "lost bird," I can't help but want to do everything in my power to help it.

MY OWN SEXUALITY has had its own journey and struggles. I wish I could say I was like my older sister and never once questioned who I was, or what I wanted. However, like everything else in my life, I didn't know anything for certain. As a young adult in high school and college, I "shopped around," as my mom called it. I dated boys. I became best friends with the gay man who I now consider my brother (cue the *Will & Grace* jokes). And I even tried dating a woman. Nothing ever seemed to fit. I spent many nights agonizing and becoming depressed because I couldn't find my place to belong.

I was practically an adult, and all the people around me were dating men, women, or both. They all seemed to know exactly what they wanted and who they were. It was an extremely difficult time of my life. My sexuality became something that I would wrestle with for the next decade. It wasn't until this past year that I realized exactly who I was. That's right, I was twenty-six before I found my identity and my place. To me that still feels odd, even though my friends tell me there is no time frame for figuring yourself out.

When I was twenty-two and still confused, I came out to Mom as a lesbian. It was a hard moment, not because I thought my mom wouldn't accept it, but because we happened to be going through a rough patch and barely speaking. You know, one of those times in your life where you think you are entirely right and your parent(s) is unfairly wrong. Either way, I decided to label myself as a lesbian at twenty-two because I wanted to fit in somewhere. I was *tired* of trying to find my place. However, about a year later, after having had my heart broken by a woman I dated, I met a boy and fell for him. That perplexed the hell out of me. I would constantly talk to my mom about my conflicted feelings. We would lay in her bed watching Meryl Streep movies and eating popcorn. She told me that it was okay to continue questioning what I truly wanted. She reminded me that she didn't decide about herself until she was about my age. That would ease my mind for a while and things would return to as normal as possible for me.

Shortly after that is when I moved to New York and the whole world of new experiences also exposed me to new ideas of identity. I was no longer confined to three definitions of my sexuality. Suddenly I was learning all these new terms: *non-binary, pansexual, asexual, transgender, demisexual, aromantic.* I was overwhelmed, but I continued to have conversations with people and I continued to learn. I expanded my mind and heart. I learned about different kinds of pronouns and how to respect different types of people within the LGBTQ+ community. And then, last summer, the serendipitous happened, and it opened my eyes forever.

In 2016, I spent the majority of my free time going to a miniscule off-Broadway theater to repeatedly watch an obscure play titled "*Straight.*" The premise was that a man was in love with both a woman and a man. His character felt the need to define himself as one or the other. He ended up making the decision he felt was more socially acceptable and not what his heart actually coveted. The play resonated with me and broke my heart. The characters found their way into my soul, and they will reside there forever.

Once afterwards, I had conversations with the lead actor. He helped me see that I knew exactly who I was after all. I am just me—nothing more, nothing less.

A second epiphany happened concurrently. I discovered I actually did have a sexual identity I could relate to. I can say with confidence I am *asexual*. Another ace friend of mine helped me realize that.

Despite that, I am no longer restricting myself to quaint, cozy labels for who I am. I am not just one thing. I am many things. I am constantly changing. Change is *good*. If we stay the same, we never grow and we never learn. I am always down for learning lots of new things. My mind is permanently open and my heart is ready to love.

At this point in my life there are a few things I know for certain:

I am loved. I can accept love from others. I can give love. I do not look down on any one person for being outside "the norm." I no longer believe normal exists. I am an adopted Italian. I am the daughter of two strong and loving women. I am a small-town girl living in a big city. My life will never be the same as my peers and that is *okay*. I am a teacher. I have a passion for children and making people smile. My name is Mary, and I am *me*.

TWO HENS AND A CHICK: MY TEENAGE LIFE WITH TWO MOMS

MIKAYLA DENAULT, age 15

KNOCK, KNOCK!

My moms, Missy and Meg, peek through the door to find the stork holding a package that awaits them on July 11, 2002.

"Any last guesses?" Meg asks as she opens the door.

As the stork looks down at the package information, he proclaims, "I have a baby delivery with the name of Peter or Mikayla with an additional request of surprise gender for Melissa Denault and Margar—Wait. You *both* are the mothers?"

Both moms look at the mail stork with confidence, and the bird gives in and uncovers a baby girl, Mikayla, bound with blankets. She glances at her new mothers with a gleaming smile that seems to say, "Of course I have two moms, why wouldn't I?"

While the baby melts her new parents' hearts, the impudent stork ruins the heartfelt moment by boldly placing a packet in their hands and stating, "Our organization has standard procedures for every LGBTQ+ couple to follow. Fill this out as quickly as possible so your baby can officially be yours."

This is the beginning of my life story as part of the three M's: Missy, Meg, and Mikayla.

MY NAME IS Mikayla Denault. I'm a fourteen-year-old girl, born from the womb of Missy Denault by insemination. I happen to have something "special" in my life—a second mother. No, she is not my stepmother from another father, and no, my mom and "dad" are not divorced. I have two lesbian parents that I love with all my heart, and who love me just as much or maybe even more bountifully.

Our love is so mighty that we have to endure a plethora of obstacles compared to a "normal" family just to be happy in this world. Growing up in an LGBTQ+ family, I've witnessed moments of betrayal, advancements, disappointment, and happiness within our community. These experiences, which may have been troubling at the time, have molded me into the strong activist I am today—spreading awareness through my nationally published articles on The Next Family (www. thenextfamily.com).

I'm a prime example of how LGBTQ+ parents are as successful as other families. Growing up in a small country town in Maryland, you might suspect our family to be shunned by society, but the truth is, I can't imagine any other place where I would feel safer. As a child, I even attended a private Catholic school, and it was the most welcoming school I've ever been to. You might be wondering, "How did she never get bullied at school for having two moms?" To be honest, I tried to figure this out myself. I realized it was because I never found having two moms an "odd" occurrence, and I made it such a frequent and chill topic to everyone around me that it just became normal. Of course, there were a few rough snags here and there, but rather than these occasions scaring us, they made us stronger for the future.

Compared to the first time my moms visited the area we live now, our community is rising up against discrimination and is the most loving place it's ever been, and I believe the world reflects this statement as well.

It all started in 1992, on a remarkably balmy afternoon in Jamestown, New York. Secretly, Missy and Meg's friends were attempting to play matchmaker. This led to my moms attending a softball practice—unbeknownst to them, they were about to meet their soulmate. As they both stepped onto the field, their hearts fluttered out of their bodies and into each other. It was love at first sight.

From that point, everything was like a dream until they realized their love meant telling their parents they're gay. Meg had an especially troubling time, growing up in a strict Irish Catholic family that supported a lot of the church's beliefs. After telling their mothers and fathers, Meg was unfortunately forced by her mother to see a psychiatrist. Thankfully after these moments, Meg and her mother were able to forgive each other, but it still silently breaks her heart when she reflects back. As the good times continued on, Meg and Missy moved to Berlin, Maryland, in 1998. Even though they were hesitant about the move, it became one of the best decisions of their lives. After I arrived in 2002, it took twelve years until Maryland finally came to its senses and allowed same-sex marriages. Missy and Meg promptly married on May 24, 2014.

The wedding day was one of the best days of my life. That day proved to the world that *love* is *love*, and it made our family feel special rather than disgraceful. We were celebrated for being a perfect, beautiful family that is always caring and kind to everyone we meet. Our motto is, "Make our positivity shine to surpass any hate." That day I was determined to make it just about them (especially since I already picked out their dresses, cake, and rings), but they did not want that to be the case.

The ceremony was at their favorite restaurant, and I was standing on stage, all smiles until Reverend Knepp called for me to stand in between Missy and Meg. Still unaware as to what was happening, I began to hysterically cry, as did the whole audience. He then opened up a box with a ring for me. *For me!* And during that moment, it smacked me—I knew our love is infinite and family is the most important thing to me in my life. Naturally, my parents had to tease me in some way, so I had to play the piano right after. I could not read any of the notes because my eyes were filled with salty water. While I was playing, the love guided me through the song like a guardian angel. We were finally able to celebrate with our true friends that had supported us through everything.

I BELIEVE THE secret to happiness is finding people that love you, will support you through everything, will be with you to try new experiences, and will share your values. As an LGBTQ+ family, we go through many moments as one unit and rise and fall together. I have so many memories with my parents that molded me into the strong person I am today. Every memory is the best and worthwhile if I'm with my moms. Memories such as attending a Pride march, picking out their wedding rings, celebrating my parents' anniversary, and answering that one reoccurring question, "You have two moms?".

Instead of just believing and hoping that the world is changing, I was able to witness it in my own backyard. Recently, on the beach near my house, the seniors of my high school planned an inspirational equality march for Pride month. About fifty people attended, and it was one of the most uplifting moments in my life. Missy, Meg, and I walked resiliently hand-in-hand. We were so grateful that we only had to deal with a couple judgmental people. There had to be at least forty others taping our celebration and joining in. The Pride march was a symbol of love in its truest form, and as mostly teenagers were strutting down the boardwalk, I'm convinced the future generation will save the world from this endless cycle of hostility.

Another nostalgic moment comes from a family-bonding vacation in the Caribbean. Just as we thought the trip couldn't get better, we stopped by an International Diamonds jewelry store for fun right after snorkeling. When Meg went to the restroom, I whispered to Missy just as a joke, "You guys should pick out your rings today since Maryland finally passed same-sex marriage!" As I'm the enforcer of the family (just kidding . . . well, not really), I got the jeweler to help me pick out my favorite rings for both of them. When I showed them to my mothers, not only were they surprised, but they surprised me by actually buying them! My favorite part of this story was that their love spread like wildfire in the whole jewelry store and the employees offered refreshments to have a big celebration. This moment proves that love has the same power in every couple and family in this universe; no love is superior to another.

The last of my favorite childhood memories centers around the popular question, "How do you have two moms?" Unlike others, I love when I hear this query because I have the opportunity to spread awareness and let them know it's not strange or sinful. When I was little, my line in response was, "I'm a miracle!" Obviously, I had no clue how I was brought forth into this world. I now hope to inspire other people to do the same, helping to build more positive memories in the future. Those events in my life strengthened my family to be unstoppable against opposition, especially since we would do anything for each other no matter what.

Currently, my family's love is ablaze stronger than ever in our hearts. About two months ago, Meg brought planks of wood home one day. Wondering what they were for, I asked her about their purpose in front of Missy. Quickly, she brought me into a separate room, saying that the wood planks were for a surprise anniversary party for Missy. They were then used to create a dance floor. Meg and I worked together as a team keeping the secret from my mom, designing the dance floor, inviting family and friends, and finally, keeping her away from the backyard on the day of the party. When all the family surprised Missy, she finally got to see the amazing dance floor. Scattered across the canvas were multicolored hearts in the order of the rainbow. I love how my family professes our unique attributes to everyone we know. The only way we are going to reach equality and end discrimination is by *awareness*.

HOWEVER, AMID THE rainbows of life, there are always thunderstorms that try to prevent us from reaching happiness and goals. As an LGBTQ+ family, we have extra storms to endure in order for us to be happy and similar to a "normal" family. To have full acceptance at my school, I had to weather some hate in the beginning. One parent did not want me to hang out with her child in pre-kindergarten. She treated me as if I were contaminated. Even though there were grosser, snot-nosed children in that class that actually seemed contaminated, no. She had to go after *my* family.

The reason why I greatly compliment the school is because my teacher fought back against the mother, and nothing of the sort ever happened again. Those teachers shielded me like they were my parents, and I will forever be grateful.

Before I was born, my moms faced negativity as well. During a trip in which they were deciding where the best place was to start a family, they decided to check out our current town. As the two were strolling down the boardwalk, not even so much as holding hands, people immediately stereotyped them and threw hateful slurs. When they told me about this, I was absolutely dumbfounded, because our area is totally different now. There are so many LGBTQ+ people in my school and community that people don't even notice it anymore.

Although I've gone through a few trials and tribu-lations, they are nothing compared to the positive feedback we receive, and I believe that our family is creating a legacy of making every family equal.

I attribute my ability to achieve greatness in my life to my moms laying a solid foundation of education, athletics, and morals. I have become an intelligent, kind-hearted young woman. Ignorant people might believe that kids who don't have traditional families or lives won't do well in life. In actuality, there is research that proclaims that children with same-sex parents are happier, healthier, and overall more successful.[1] Why, you ask? I believe it's because the parents are more prepared, making sure the pregnancy or adoption goes perfectly and no one can take away their child, even if some people still want to take away their rights. Also, almost 100% of children with LGBTQ+ parents are deliberate, not accidents.

I swim on a team six days a week, write for a national blog, take an engineering class, act in theater, do triathlons, run cross-country, work on computer design, and I have been receiving straight As for seven years consecutively. If those are not accomplishments, tell me, what are? I am confident that children with LGBTQ+ parents gain their determination from their parents because those parents work extra vigorously just to keep their children protected from discrimination, violence, and the government.

If it weren't for my parents' involvement in my life, I don't believe that I would have as many true friends as I do now. Missy and Meg changed the rule of

---

1 https://www.theguardian.com/australia-news/2017/oct/23/children-raised-by-same-sex-parents-do-as-well-as-their-peers-study-shows

LGBTQ+ couples being different in my community by volunteering in sports around the area. Missy created a whole sports program in our beachfront community. She was the head coach of basketball, soccer, swim team, and others. She loved those experiences so much, she expanded to the YMCA. There, her main priority is making sure children are fully optimizing their time to live happy, healthy and accomplished lives. Every week, she teaches children swim lessons so they can be relaxed and safe in the water.

Meg also volunteered as a coach with Missy. In the mornings, Missy would study with me, while Meg would check my homework at night. Before I was born, Meg read every baby book known to humanity to make sure I would be granted the best atmosphere. For my early education, she found Leap Frog; this was obviously the best option for me. My moms are the best because they are generous with me and my community, in an effort to make the world a better place filled with peace. Even if they sometimes don't receive the same in return.

As THE FUTURE looms ominously over our heads, we have to continue spreading love against the negativity. In the years to come, I hope to become an even more influential activist for the LGBTQ+ society and their rights. I want to influence people with my writing, teaching how to love everyone no matter what gender, race, ethnicity, or sexual orientation they are. When I enter college in three years, I want to show my parents all that I have learned from them and prove that they are the best family I could ever ask for on the face of this planet. Together we can achieve greatness, but also on my own I can shine a light illuminated by my parents for everyone to follow into truth and happiness.

The question that you all have been wondering has been answered: "How are the lives of children in LGBTQ+ families?"

The truth is, almost exactly the same as every other child; we just have to work a little bit harder. I am as loved as any other kid in the world—maybe even more so. I am blessed to have such a supportive community and have had so many experiences, both good and bad, that I am able to take with me while going into future endeavors. Living in an LGBTQ+ family is worth the criticism because you get to meet amazing people with inspirational backgrounds.

LGBTQ+ families are some of the strongest people in the world when we spread awareness and create peace. As my family shares all it can with others, our joy and love will spread across the world in a chain reaction, changing society as we know it. Love is stronger than any power in the world. Without it, civilization would fall apart.

My two moms have been the most important part of my life, health, and love. Living with them has resulted in me having more confidence, kindness, pride, respect, and hope than my peers. I believe that with my moms, with my family and friends supporting us, we can break many barriers that have yet to be broken in order for all of us to reach everlasting peace.

THE WOMAN WHO ~~CANNOT~~ REFUSES TO FRENCH BRAID HER HAIR

EMILY GRUBBS, age 21

I HAVE ABSOLUTELY no clue how to French braid my hair. I don't know how to French braid *any* hair, for that matter. As a twenty-one-year-old grown woman, I simply cannot twist and style my tresses into the particular fashion that results in a *Proper. French. Braid.* But all women are inherently supposed to know how to French braid, right?

I grew up in Canton, Ohio—the epitome of hetero-normative, white, upper-middle-class suburbia. I was an awkward prepubescent girl, feeling envious of my girlfriends. They could braid the hell out of hair: their dolls' hair, my hair, their own hair. As I matured, the list of essential feminine skills I lacked grew—I didn't know how to put eyeliner on, I didn't know how to dye my hair, I still don't know how to properly apply eye shadow. I'm a failure; as a woman, I fail. At least, that is what society tells me.

If you don't live under a rock, or a massive pile of systemic propaganda, then you've probably heard that gender is just a social construct. Along with sexuality, race, marriage, family, etc., gender is just another fictitious set of categories shaped by social hierarchy and privilege. I am told by society, led to believe, that because I do not know how to properly demonstrate and display my femininity, I am a flawed woman. As I developed my own version of the female identity, I watched other girls my age and I wondered why I was so different. What I didn't know at the time is how deeply grateful I would be that I didn't, and never will, fit into the perfect mold society has designed for me.

Being raised by lesbian parents is different, life-altering, magical, difficult, eye-opening, painful. When people ask me—which they always inevitably do—what it was like being brought up by a same-sex couple, I have a well-prepared answer. I tell them about my amazing childhood, filled with happy memories and pure childish wonder. I tell them that my moms taught me how to be a kind and accepting person, in a way that has made me uniquely empathetic. I tell them that I am now an aspiring human rights activist and my passion directly stems from my upbringing.

Often, when I tell the story of having lesbian parents, I focus on the positive; I stick to the version I want the public to understand. I feel certain that every person I share my story with helps destroy the false narrative that history has told. Everything I've explained to people has been true and genuine, but it is not the *complete* narrative. What I don't tell the world is how being raised by two moms is hard. Anyone who has been bullied knows how painful it is to be different. Our society does not take kindly to those who do not represent the white, heteronormative, able-bodied, rich, cismale narrative; an "ideal" construct so many people don't fit into. Being parented by a lesbian couple has made me incredibly strong, but building that strength was no simple task.

My best friend growing up was named Rebecca. She and I originally *hated* each other in the fourth grade because we were competing for a mutual friend's attention. It wasn't until our mutual friend moved away that we realized that we were better off being companions rather than adversaries. So she and I became best pals, and when it came time for my eleventh birthday, it was entirely expected that she would attend my party. However, there was one problem—her mom would not allow her to come to my house. Rebecca was raised in a strictly Christian home, which, according to her mom, was not conducive with my homosexual household. So, my moms had the onus of explaining to me why my bestie would not be at my eleventh birthday party. Try to imagine having to tell your eleven-year-old child that their closest companion can't come to their birthday party, just because of who you are and whom you love.

Attempting to explain discrimination to your child is painful, feeling discriminated against is painful, and it is especially painful for a young child who wants nothing more than to share her birthday with her best friend. I can only imagine what my moms felt in that moment—sadness, fury, guilt. Being LGBTQ+ is not a choice, but deciding who you allow into your life is. When I think back on this story now, I feel bad for Rebecca. I feel pity when I think about all the love and acceptance she missed out on because of her family's intolerance. I am grateful for my ability to empathize with her now; that is what having homosexual parents is like. Having same-sex parents makes me the bigger person, but I am forced to be the bigger person. What I don't always tell people about this story is that I also feel bad for eleven-year-old me. I feel bad for the girl who struggled to make friends and was forced to try to understand, if it is even possible to understand at that age, why she was too different, wrong, "perverted" to have her best friend at her party.

This story is filled with pain—my moms' pain of not being able to give their child what she wants most, my pain of not having my best friend at my birthday party, Rebecca's pain of not being able to attend and not truly understanding why, and Rebecca's mom's pain, at least I would imagine that she felt some—being hateful must cause some pain. This story is not all rainbows and unicorns, and neither is being raised by LGBTQ+ parents. Being labeled as "abnormal" in our society leads to hurtful and isolating experiences. I hope that by sharing some of my own stories someone else will find solace and camaraderie with my struggle, because while pain demands to be felt, the hurt can be softened if you have people to help you heal.

My moms chose to send me to an extremely small Montessori school. While it taught me how to be independent, ambitious, and thoughtful, it also isolated me socially. By the time I graduated in the eighth grade, I was one of ten graduates. So, it is understandable that I ran into confrontation when I was forced to venture out of my comfort zone. I can still remember when I had to start riding the bus home in fourth grade. At the time, riding the bus was Guantanamo-esque torture.

Since my Montessori school was so small, we shared buses with the local Catholic school. I rode it with my little brother and we both just tried our best to ignore the "bad" kids who would sit at the rear end of the bus. In reality, we were the nerds who sat at the front of the bus, while everyone who sat in the back was considered cool or popular.

One thing I have found to be true about many popular kids, especially during adolescence, is that they can be unbelievably cruel. Being sheltered by the Montessori environment led to me being quite shell-shocked when I started riding the bus. The kids from the Catholic school were ruthless. Perhaps it was the conservative environment they were being forced into, but by the time they made it on the bus after school, they were determined to be as deviant and obnoxious as possible. I was already weird, awkward, chubby, and nerdy, and I was certainly not going to give my barbarous peers more ammunition by sharing that I had lesbian parents. The last thing I needed was a bunch of conservative preteens teasing me about my LGBTQ+ upbringing. I remember being able to maintain isolation and go undetected for a while, until my brother blew our cover.

My brother was approximately six at the time, so I obviously cannot blame him for spilling the rainbow beans; he was too young to know that having gay parents was considered "wrong." As I recall it, one day my brother unwittingly shouted to the entire bus: "I don't have a dad, I have two moms!"

Now, there are two versions of this story from this point:

THE FIRST ONE: The biggest bully on the bus, a

hyperactive sixth grader with a Bieber bowl-cut, started teasing my brother. "Wait! What do you mean, you have two moms? Your parents are gay, like really gay? That probably means you're gay, too. I bet you're a faggot." Unfortunately, my brother was short, innocent, and eccentric, so an association with homosexuality did not serve him well with the insecure, budding alpha males on the bus. When Bieber-bully started taunting my little brother I had to act, so I stood up and told him, "Shut up and stop being a jerk!" I added, "Having gay parents does not make you gay, it makes you a good person— having gay parents makes you the kind of person that would stand up against a bully like you!"

THE SECOND ONE: Is what actually happened. When the kids on the bus, (including Bieber-bully) started teasing my brother, I just grabbed him and told him to be quiet. I told him that he should just not tell everyone he has two moms. I explained that some people don't understand that our family is different, and that's okay—some people are just mean. We essentially shoved ourselves in the closet, hidden and ashamed.

Admittedly, I have told the first version of the story as if that is what actually happened. In truth, I wish I had stood up to that bully; I would have shown my brother, and all those kids on that bus, that having lesbian parents is not wrong and they all would have been better for it. Instead, I told my brother to keep his head low and hide who he is. In that moment, I was embarrassed. I felt having LGBTQ+ parents was wrong.

However, sometimes when I am feeling particularly reflective, I think that what I did that day was *not* so disappointing. How can I have expected myself, at the innocent age of ten, to be able to stand up for LGBTQ+ rights in front of a bus-full of my judgmental peers? Being a member of the LGBTQ+ community does not make you inherently strong; it's the community and the reliance that builds your strength. On that day on the bus so many years ago, I did not act with strength. Rather, I acted out of fear and shame, but at least I was not the villain.

After writing this chapter and reflecting more on this event, I brought it up to my brother, to see what he remembered. In response, he told me a very different story that happened many years later. I was already in high school, and he was left to fend for himself and my little sister on the treacherous bus. He explained that one day during eighth grade, the rainbow beans flowed again and Bieber-bully version 2.0 was teasing him and my younger sister about having lesbian parents. In my brother's version of the story, he went up to that kid and socked him a good one, right in the face.

Now, please do not read this as a condonation of violence—we cannot just all go around punching people who treat us unfairly. While my brother could have found a more peaceful way to express his feelings, the brother I was so scared to defend grew up to defend himself and the LGBTQ+ community at large. My moms created another LGBTQ+ warrior.

While he chose in that moment to use his fists as weapons, I try to act as a better example by using words as my ammunition. Every word I write is another shot against the heteronormative defense. I felt such shame for not defending my brother so many years ago, but for every singular moment I hesitated to stand up for my beliefs, there are infinite examples of courage that over-shadow momentary doubts. What my brother's story proves to me is that I did show him how to stand up for himself. Maybe that day on the bus—so many years ago—when I couldn't stand up to the original Bieber-Bully, is just a blip on the greater narrative I created for my siblings. I am a warrior, my brother is a warrior, and my little sister is now off to defeat Bieber-Bully Version 3.0, until there are no more evolutions.

Having lesbian parents means that you empathize with the oppressed, rather than the oppressor. Moreover, here I am today writing my story for the world to judge, and that takes tremendous courage. Having two moms has forced me to grow into a strong and outspoken person. Today I would not hesitate to challenge and educate *any* bully. I am not afraid of *any* oppressor. They are the real tragedy, *they* are the ones who are so fragile that they need to bring other people down in order to build them-selves up. I wonder, if more kids were raised by LGBTQ+ parents maybe there would not be so many bullies in the world. Hopefully we'll find out some day.

AFTER I GRADUATED from Montessori school, I entered the real word—high school. Well, "entered" is too mild of a word—crashed, careened, plummeted, might be more appropriate descriptions. I went from a class of ten to a class of five hundred. I was a hyper-nerdy, over-weight, awkward fourteen-year-old and I knew no one. Accordingly, for the first week of school I ate my lunch in the bathroom and longed for some friends.

My transition into high school was influenced by a plethora of factors, but having lesbian parents was definitely an important portion of my identity, whether I wanted it to be or not. During my freshman year, whenever I elected to tell someone I had two moms, I was terrified they would reject me. At the time, all I wanted was to be socially accepted, and having same-sex parents does not fall into the "socially accepted" category. As to be expected, I faced bullying in high school; in this day and age I think every young person has played the role of both bully and bullied at least once. However, having lesbian parents made me realize that ultimately, I pity the bully more than the bullied.

The truth is that teenagers are mean and know exactly where and when to strike. Once I was enlisted into the battlefield of high school, I started to realize just how different my family was compared to my peers. My classmates were fascinated by my existence—they looked at me as an oddity, something to study, an "other." Everyone wanted to ask politically incorrect and oftentimes rude questions about my family. Some of which included: "So, like which one is the man? How did they have you? So you *have* to have a dad, right?" And the ever-present: "Are *you* gay?" At the time I was happy to get any attention from my peers so I indulged them with the answers they sought.

I was confident in my upbringing—I knew I had fantastic parents—so I exploited their lesbianism for some attention. When I was in high school, I initially identified as straight, which made talking about my parents easier. I was just seen as an extremely dedicated, straight ally. According to society, I *personally* was not deviant, but I had ample insight into the elusive world of homosexuality. However, the thing about sharing one's personal life with anyone who asks (especially in high school) is that people gossip and rumors spread.

It wasn't long until my new friends informed me that there were rumors floating around that *I* was a lesbian. Hypocritically, I was very upset when I discovered people were associating me with my parents. I realized I could no longer control my narrative—simply telling people I was straight was not enough. My identity was being shaped by my peers and I started to lose sight of who I was. Being labeled as a lesbian was akin to being labeled undesirable. I was always so physically insecure, the last thing I needed was to be labeled the weird, fat, lesbian. "How would a boy ever like me?"

My solution was to come out as bisexual. While I really was attracted to girls, my main focus was rebranding myself. I thought: *Boys love girls who kiss other girls and kiss them, right? Being bisexual is sexier than being a lesbian, right?* Again, rumors flourished. My new girlfriends started to inquire if I was attracted to them. I got pointlessly slut-shamed. So many of my peers simply did not *believe* me. Upon reflection, I didn't even understand what my own story was.

I can still starkly remember one day when I was leaving school. I received an anonymous voicemail that contained five minutes of the nastiest insults high school girls could concoct. I listened in shock as I was repeatedly called "a fugly dyke." I was told that "just because I "had big tits" did *not* mean I was "sexy," and that I was "just a fat, desperate whore." Since my mom was picking me up, I broke down instantly when I got into the car. I remember feeling so violated and vulnerable. Why did someone hate me this much? What did I do to deserve their malice? What was *wrong* with me?

The problem with bullying, especially at tender ages, is that it makes the bullied feel like *they* have done wrong or have something inherently bad about them. I now know that when my peers told me that being bisexual made me both a "fugly dyke" and a "desperate whore," they were just expressing their *own* insecurities. However at the time, all I wanted was to change myself so they would like me.

After enough rejection, I redacted my bisexuality and suppressed my identity for the sake of my classmates' approval. It was not until college that I felt comfortable coming out as queer. Now, as a senior in my undergraduate career, I have connected with men, women, and non-binary partners and feel proud and assured in my sexuality. I believe that sexuality is a large part of a person's identity, and while society made me afraid to be myself at first, having lesbian parents has given me the permission to be whoever I want to be.

Having same-sex parents ultimately creates a deep dichotomy between the limitations society tries to put on you, and the freedom their openness gifts you. My young life was spent fighting against society, while desperately trying to fit in. Now I have never felt more sure of who I am—I know I love myself, and I will never be afraid to love whomever I choose.

AFTER MY FIRST couple years in high school, my peers became more accepting of my status as a lesbian offspring. Once I started being proud of my moms and not allowing myself to be bullied, I gained some mild respect from my classmates. I slowly became known as an outspoken

LGBTQ+ activist, and most people tolerated my pride. I found that even my more conservative and religious friends were considerably progressive—they would say, "Being gay is a sin, but . . . everyone sins."

That sentiment is not at all what I personally believe, and is not the narrative I would promote or accept, but it allowed me to feel more comfortable with people of that ilk. I policed my peers when they would use homophobic language, to the point that my friends became annoyed. When that happened, it never bothered me, because their annoyance was, and still is, far exceeded by the pain that LGBTQ+ people feel when they hear or are called derogatory terms.

By the time I reached junior year, we started covering some politically relevant content in class, and of course gay rights was a hot topic. Some of my friends warned me of the looming subject, after they had the discussion in an earlier block of my class. They also revealed to me that during their forum, one of our classmates spoke openly about his opinion that kids raised by gay parents could not possibly understand love. I remember this so distinctly because it was such a direct target at my existence that I started to question myself: *I am kid raised by gay parents and I don't know anything about love.*

In hindsight, I realize my confusion about love was not due to my lesbian moms, but rather my status as an awkward sixteen-year-old. I knew that outspoken kid who thought I was an abomination, and I was not sure how to react. Part of me wanted to just respect his right to share his opinion (probably a lesson intended by the exercise), but I was not going to let my position go undefended.

When my time to debate finally arrived, I was loaded and ready to fire at anyone who tried to offer any homophobic comments. However, when it started, not a single one of my peers had anything negative to say about LGBTQ+ marriage and rights—not *one*. In my opinion, a room full of high school juniors in complete consensus that LGBTQ+ people should, of course, have equal rights is pretty remarkable and hope-inducing. I'd like to think that maybe I had an influence on some of them that day. I suspect some of them were too uncomfortable to openly share any homophobic thoughts in front of the kid who has lesbian moms. Good.

What the debate, or lack thereof, proved to me is that every time I "annoyed" my peers by condemning their homophobic language and ideas, I was making an impression on them. I didn't have to fight against homophobia that day, because I had been fighting it since the day I was born. Maybe neither I nor my peers realized it, but my continual nagging and defiance was enough to shut down any potential homophobic comments in that debate. I was so used to having the wrong or unpopular opinion, I had not even considered that maybe my position had become the norm. On that day, my peers felt *ashamed* about their homophobia and I felt *proud* representation of the LGBTQ+ community. I look forward to the day that LGBTQ+ rights won't even be a debatable topic.

AFTER FINISHING MY submission for this publication, I shared my essay with my moms. I was so excited to hear their reactions, but I was surprised when they responded with confusion and heartbreak. While I did not expect their reaction, I have come to understand their sadness. The stories of my personal suffering were not easy for my moms to read; they did not know the extent of the bullying I faced. After internalizing their response, I started to wonder how others would react to my story. Would potential same-sex parents fear having children after reading about the torment I faced?

While I do not have children of my own, I do have younger siblings whom I worry and care about. Recently, one of my moms called to discuss some concerns about my little sister. What I came to realize during our conversation is that my sister is currently facing the same torment I did so many years ago. My mother explained that my sister has been taunted by her fellow classmates about her sexuality, and I couldn't help but empathize. I know exactly what it feels like to have your peers manipulate and judge your identity. In a time when my sister is in such a fragile state, I wish I could just tuck her away and protect her from the world. I think that is the root of the sadness my moms feel about my past experiences—they just wish they could have protected and shielded me from my pain. However, what my parents, and all future same-sex parents, need to realize is complete protection is not possible, or even ideal. Reality is cold, but it is *inevitable*.

After hearing about my sister's struggles with bullying, I asked her about being tormented. She was quick to tell me that it is the bullies who are wrong, not her; "*I would* never *want to be like the mean kids*." What these "mean kids" don't know is that my sister is the third evolution of the LGBTQ+ warrior and her strength is fueled by compassion and support.

My sister told me about the myriad of friends she has made, because of their shared, marginalized identity. She described her best friend, a young boy coming to terms with his own sexuality. She told me about the two sisters she befriended after she saw them being harassed by her peers for their Syrian-refugee status. While I worry about my sister, she is growing not only into an LGBTQ+ warrior, but a combatant for social justice and equality, for all people who feel isolated from society.

Although the bullying I faced caused me pain, I would not go back in time to erase my suffering; this is what I want all current and future same-sex parents to understand. From great adversity comes great strength. I would not be the strong, independent woman I am today without the harassment of my past bullies. While I am inclined to feel sad about my sister's struggles, I try instead to imagine the kind of powerful woman she is growing to be. I am confident that my gentle-natured sister will make it through this dark time, and she will come out of it callused and transformed. LGBTQ+ Warrior 3.0.

AS AN ACADEMIC, I feel compelled to take some time to reflect on the sociological and political repercussions of having same-sex parents. Having two moms allowed me to view gender in a completely different way than most of the people in our society. I was primarily shaped by strong female role-models, so I was never originally taught that a man was the "societal ideal." The patriarchy could not touch the development of my understanding of gender, at least for a little while. It was not until the world showed me its ugly head, shaped by discrimination, systemic inequality, and power, that I released what it means to be viewed as a woman in our society. I was shielded by the power of my mothers.

My moms are both very successful in their own right. Their success and achievement taught me that, as a woman, I am fully capable of achieving any goal I strive for. Currently, I am truly thriving and reaching for the stars. I feel no burden to have children or settle down. I know that I can beat out any man for the job I desire, and I am not ashamed of my "masculine personality."

I took a quiz the other day on Facebook (which, clearly is a highly reputable source) and it told me that, based on my own assessment of my personality traits, I am approximately 93% masculine. Shocker. While I was not surprised by my results, I started to question myself yet again. I was transported right back to my younger self. *Does this Facebook quiz know I still can't French braid my hair?*

So, does this just mean I was meant to be a guy? No, of course not! What it means is that despite the fact that I feel biologically empowered as a woman, I simply do not fit the social construct for a female gender-role. I *shatter* the damned glass ceiling. I *refuse* to let society tell me what kind of woman I have to be. I want to be *strong*—both physically and emotionally.

I can't even count the number of men who have told me I intimidate them and, at first, it bothered me quite a bit. Sometimes I still get insecure and think, "Can I get a man to love me if I scare them all away with my independence, intelligence, and confidence?" And then I remember that any man who does not want a strong and severe woman does not deserve one. Besides, who needs insecure men when you are queer?

What does all this amount to? Where is the lesson to be drawn? Can LGBTQ+ parents raise kids? I don't think I can answer those questions and I do not intend to. My intention with my story is to shed light on my "non-normative experience." My hope is that people will read this story and connect to it. I want to prove that *anyone* can relate to my experiences. All people experience pain, rage, shame, and fear.

Part of being human is feeling confused about one's identity and sexuality. I am sharing my experiences because of their very abnormal nature, but I think where there is variance there is also similarity. Having lesbian parents intrinsically shaped the person I am today, and will continue to influence my life. Still, there are countless other factors that make me who I am. Ultimately, my moms gave me the freedom to be anyone I want to be and I am quite proud to be a woman who simply cannot French braid her hair.

MY DAD IS A DRAG . . . QUEEN

RYAN MURPHY, age 18

FIRST, I DON'T think of my dad as a "gay dad." He has always been just "my dad." Nothing is different because this is all I've ever known. No matter the situation, he's always been a dad *first*—he never let anything get in the way of that. He drove me to school, made my lunch, bought me clothes, made sure I was happy and healthy, and did his best to raise me just as any parent would. Personally, I like to think he did a pretty damn good job. He's taught me right from wrong, that everybody's equal and deserves respect, and if you have the opportunity to help somebody, it is your responsibility to help them. A lot of parents could actually take notes from him—I genuinely believe that.

Yes, I have a mom—that's usually the first question people ask when I initially explain my family situation. They met in the mid-90s working at a jewelry store in the mall—coincidentally, the same mall I work at now. My dad knew he was gay, and my mom did as well. However, they both felt an inexplicable attraction for each other, and their friends all told them to go for it.

So, they were married in 1996, and I was born two years later. My mom, Lynn, had a son from a previous marriage, my half brother, Kyle.

We all co-existed happily together until about 2004, when my parents separated but still lived together. My mom started talking to my brother's dad again, and they are now married and live in Tampa. I still see her often, and talk to her almost every day. She has played a significant role in my life, but I've lived with my dad for eight years now. My mom influenced me as far as music and art, but my dad is definitely the one who raised and instilled values in me.

The night my dad came out of the closet, he pulled me aside from watching TV and sat me down in my bedroom. He began reluctantly, "You know I'll always love you, nothing will change that." And then he looked me in the eyes and confided in me, "I'm gay."

To which I, at eleven years old, responded with, "I don't care, let's go watch TV." It just wasn't something that was a big deal to me. Even at that age, I knew plenty of my dad's friends who were gay, and it never felt strange.

My childhood was relatively normal, save the numerous drag shows I attended. I had lots of friends, sleepovers, hobbies, and all the usual social interaction a hetero-parental counterpart would have. As far back as sixth grade, my friends have always been supportive and I've never heard anything negative from people who know my dad is gay. When he first came out to me, he suggested I not go telling everybody just yet...but that's exactly what I did, and all my friends thought it was cool! For my dad, it was monumental to witness kids from this generation be so accepting. It's a lot different now than it was thirty years ago. It made him incredibly happy to see that I was still proud of him.

He raised me to be open-minded because, well, it's the way one should be, but also because he knew he would eventually have to come out to me. I couldn't be happier with my life. I see people who look down on every aspect of the LGBTQ+ community and it hurts me. If only those bigots knew how wonderful a dad I have, and how protective he is of me. Whenever he starts talking to a guy, he brings them around me before anything gets serious to see if I approve and to gauge if they are comfortable with me. If either of those are problems, my dad stops seeing them immediately.

WHEN I WAS about twelve years old, my dad took me to my first Pride festival. I knew most of the performers, and they knew me. too. I was dressed up in a head-to-toe neon green morph-suit topped off with a rainbow afro wig, and I couldn't have been more comfortable. I walked around and took pictures with tons of people, talked with people about me and my dad, and I had a fantastic time. I saw no one angry—only smiling faces, happy friends, and families. I saw dozens of extravagant drag queens and entertainers, beautiful hairstyles and dresses and art—it really does open your mind up to a whole new world of culture. Everybody felt accepted. You didn't have to worry about being made fun of, because it was such a loving and tolerant environment. I wish everybody could experience it at least once in their life, but sadly many people are too close-minded.

I've never felt uncomfortable with myself because I

was raised to not worry about what other people think. I paint my nails, and dye my hair whatever color I want—it's currently hot pink. My dad has been telling me for years, "It doesn't matter what other people think." And really, why should it? The only opinion that matters is your own. Just do your best to be happy, healthy and helpful. That's how we've always lived. A lot of my peers might be afraid to express themselves because their friends might not like it, or their parents may not approve, but I've never worried about that. All of my friends are just as open-minded as I am, and if they aren't, I will always help them get there.

Upon reflection, the main difference I notice about myself is that I'm much more open than most kids my age, whether it be socially, mentally, or culturally. I can talk to anyone about anything, no matter skin color, gender, sexual orientation or musical taste—I do not judge. I enjoy a wider range of music and cinema than most do. My dad is a huge fan of 80s pop and disco (imagine that), and I've discovered that I have a particular fondness for it, too. Some of my favorite movies are *Whatever Happened to Baby Jane*, *To Wong Foo Thanks for Everything, Julie Newmar*, and *Mommie Dearest*. Not your typical flicks by any means. I am open to things and experiences that I might not have been if I had a traditional upbringing.

Okay, well maybe there is *one* more difference. My dad has been a drag queen since the 1980s and has become renowned throughout Florida. He used to have a show at the largest nightclub in Florida every Saturday night for years. His drag name is Morgan Davis, though he's also known as "The Glitter Queen" because he doesn't shave his beard—he covers it in glitter to match his hair, outfit and makeup. I've had friends (and a girl-friend or two) witness him in drag in person before, and they adored him/her. I'm not afraid to show off pictures, and I love when people ask me about it. A couple of his favorite songs to perform are "Boobs" by Ruth Wallis, and "The Pussycat Song," by Connie Vannett. He plays the tracks in his car constantly, and all the words are permanently embedded into my brain.

I've met so many beautiful and amazing people because of my dad's drag persona, and it's had a very large impact on who I am as a person today. I've never been embarrassed or felt shame about this part of his life. So far, nobody has said anything rude to us and we are both so fortunate to have not received any nega-tivity. Not many people are as fortunate as us.

I remember once, a couple of years ago, my dad and I were at our local grocery store. We had been coming to this store for years—our last two homes were less than five minutes away. The staff all knew us, but they didn't know about my dad's drag life. It was a Sunday afternoon, the day after his weekly show. He paid the cashier, who knows us by name and sees us every week, in his tip money, which had to have been at least $30 in crumpled up, glittery $1 bills. The cashier joked, "Are you a dancer?" To which my dad replied, "Close, but no, I'm an entertainer." She looked puzzled, and asked, "What do you mean by that?" My dad promptly looked around and took out his phone. He didn't say anything, he just showed her a picture. She loved it and asked if she could show another employee. Of course my dad said yes; he didn't mind, he never does. Meeting somebody like my dad was a first for both of them. They became Facebook friends, and even went to his shows.

I am the child of a gay parent, and am very proud of it. I'm "normal" and I have a healthy relationship with both of my parents. My dad has always been my dad first, and no circumstance will ever change that. This is how we live our lives—we don't hide anything, and if people ask, we educate them. We openly talk about our lives and our experiences, and we want people to know that there's nothing wrong with it, and it's quite fabulous, actually.

"I KNOW YOU ARE, BUT WHAT AM I?"

LARA LILLIBRIDGE, age 44

I USED TO think I would somehow turn gay in my sleep—that I would wake up and suddenly like girls the same way that I liked boys, and I was pretty obsessed with boys. There were already little signs that it might be possible—like the tingles I felt when I saw fashion models on the covers of magazines or poised seductively on the hood of a car. In the 80s, it seemed like every magazine and billboard was festooned with cleavage and long legs. I was a tomboy who loved to ride bikes, climb trees, and beat up boys in the playground, but I made sure I kept my hair long so people knew I was a girl. Deep down, I knew that I wasn't all-girl, or at least, not an entirely straight one. But I fought it, dreaded it, and would have prayed for absolution if I had believed in God.

Before you laugh and say, "People don't just turn gay in their sleep," please know that I had evidence. Pat, my mom's partner, knew she was gay since she was twelve-years-old. Ergo, before then, she could have been just like me. My mother always said she was a "political lesbian," and if it had worked out with my father, she might never have examined her sexuality further. Since my father couldn't keep his pants zipped, they divorced, she returned to school, embraced feminism and became a lesbian. "I couldn't hold onto my own power in a relationship with a man," she explained. "I kept falling into the same subservient ways." So not only was lesbianism something that could happen at any moment, but apparently feminism was a gateway to it.

I thought becoming a lesbian was about the worst thing that could happen to someone. My brother and I were forbidden to tell anyone the truth about our family because our parents could lose their jobs. I knew that my parents were always careful to be vague about their relationship statuses at work, and if they lost their jobs, we would lose our house. Our deed even said that the house could never be sold to Blacks, Jews, homosexuals, or "other undesirables," which my parents laughed about, because we got 'em on two fronts—the gay part and the Jewish part. They reassured me that such wording was illegal, but I was smart enough to know only the race and religion parts were protected by law. The gay part was not.

I knew about gay men getting beaten to death. We got *The Empty Closet, Advocate,* and *Ms. Magazine* every month, not that I read them, but my parents did and told me what I needed to know. I already knew that being called *fag* or *queer* were the worst insults on the playground long before they were applied to me directly. In seventh grade, our family was outed by the daughter of a bisexual woman, a social acquaintance of my mother, and then "Lara the Lezzie" became my nickname at school, along with all the other permutations: *lez, lesbian, lesbo,* and even *fag,* as if the kids didn't even know the difference.

Besides, I could plainly see that my parents weren't happy people. My stepmother, Pat, was always yelling, my mother's mouth always pulled down at the corners. Pat was quick to blame anything that went wrong on her sexuality—people didn't like her? It was because she was a lesbian. Window got broken? It was because she was a lesbian. Didn't get a raise at work? Homophobia strikes again. So I had no other words to explain what was wrong with us. I wasn't given the words *mental illness, clinical depression,* or *bipolar*—words that also applied to my household, it turned out.

Now, it's not that I didn't know happy lesbians. My parents had many lesbian friends who seemed happy, fun, even well-adjusted, but I only saw them at parties, and I knew that nearly everyone was happier at parties than they were at home. I knew how hard it was to be gay, no matter how much they smiled.

WHEN I WAS seventeen I got a job at a flower shop. I was the only girl and the only hetero, but these were a different kind of queer people that I had never seen before. They didn't try to hide their sexuality, but rather exalted in it. The five gay men laughed and teased each other, called each other "Mary," and competed to see who could sound the most like a phone sex operator when they answered the shop phone. All day long, other gay men stopped by just to visit, and while our shop was always busy, it was the happiest job I ever had, even when I had to clean the toilets and mop the floors.

Gay parties were better than lesbian parties, too. My parents always had a 4th of July party, one at Christmas, and another on New Year's Eve. We always had two baskets lined with paper towels—one filled with Doritos, the other with pretzels. The silver chaffing dish was polished and filled with tiny hotdogs, a can of blue-flamed Sterno keeping them warm. On New Year's Eve they added a silver tray with disposable champagne flutes that came apart into two pieces for easy storage. When I went to my first gay party, there were flowers, candles, and gold Mylar balloons with streamers that hung to the floor. The food was displayed on risers, so everything was at a different height, and there was caviar on ice instead of little baby hotdogs over Sterno. I called my mother, feeling betrayed. "You are not really gay!" I accused her. "I just went to a party at Robert's, and there were flowers, and caviar—"

My mother interrupted my rant. "Oh, honey, you just learned the difference between gays and lesbians. Gay parties are Hollywood. Lesbian parties are Doritos in a basket."

Clearly, if one was to be homosexual, anyone could see that being gay was preferable to being a lesbian by a mile.

Then my friends started dying. The shop closed. My gay family was gone.

I MARRIED THE most masculine man I could find—a biker that played hockey and watched football. I was feminine by default. I listened to Rush Limbaugh and told everyone that I wanted to be "barefoot, pregnant, and in the kitchen," though I assumed *barefoot* was a fashion choice, not an economic one. I wanted more than anything to be just like everyone else.

I had a couple of lesbian friends of my own in my twenties, and I went to a lesbian bar or two with them, but I was the odd girl out. Even when I explained that my mother was a lesbian, I was married to a man—they could tell I wasn't one of them. This was in the 90s, before the word *ally* was in vogue. I wanted to tell them that I had been in the gay community longer than they had, but it didn't matter. I was an outsider now, and that wedding ring ensured that I would never have to wonder about turning gay ever again.

WHEN MY MOTHER turned fifty, she and Pat quit their jobs, sold the house, and bought a boat, ending up in Key West, Florida. When I was twenty-six, I got divorced and moved there as well. We went to a gay church, bingo at a gay bar, and my mother wrote a column for the gay newspaper and reviewed gay fiction for a couple of places. My mom's face started to develop laugh lines. When I told people my mom was a lesbian, they merely shrugged, as if I'd said she had brown eyes—even the straight people. No one asked me if I thought I might be a lesbian, like almost all the straight people I told back home.

Gay and lesbian parents, however, always asked me the same thing. "Will my children hate me?" I always gave the same answer: "Yes, but they would also hate you if you had an accent, were overweight, or dressed funny. They will hate you if you don't let them stay out past midnight or let their best friend spend the night on a school night. Teenagers all hate their parents at one point or another, at least for a few hours of their life."

I HAD A LESBIAN friend who was sitting in her living room with the windows open, while her thirteen-year-old son and his friend hung out on the porch outside.

"So I hear your mom is a lesbian," the boy said, and my friend froze in fear for what would happen next.

"No, my mom is *queen* of the lesbians," her son replied, and they went off to skateboard. It seemed being lesbian wasn't the problem; being closeted was.

I FOUND MY own place in the gay community—I had gay and lesbian friends my own age, not just my parents and their friends. My roommate was a drag queen, and I wouldn't leave the house unless he helped me accessorize properly. I went to gay bars and drag shows as well as the straight dance clubs. I even went to church when my parents were north for the summer and I didn't have to, because the gay community was my extended family once again.

I was at a Key West bar with my brother, and a girl my age walked by. She was one of the most beautiful women I had ever seen, and I told my brother so. For the first time, I felt like I could be attracted to girls without it being a death sentence. It was the year 2000, and people had started to believe that bisexuals actually existed, and weren't just gay people who hadn't fully come to terms with their sexuality. I kissed my first girl, then my second. I decided I still liked kissing boys better. Honestly, although I found women attractive, I still couldn't imagine a life as a lesbian. It just wasn't how I wanted my life to unfold. My place in the gay world was as an ally, and any boy who was serious about me had to prove their worth by going to gay bingo and a drag show before I'd consider them dating material.

Of course, kissing boys leads to other things, and before I turned thirty I fell in love and moved off the island to get married again. Both my moms walked me down the aisle, and my new in-laws didn't think there was anything wrong with that. My new husband and I moved to Kansas, and I kept a framed picture of my parents on my desk at work. When some people told me they'd pray for them, I only said, "thank you," pretending they said that about everyone's parents. I started contributing to LGBTQ+ charities automatically out of my paycheck every week, because it seemed the only way to reconcile it. When I confirmed that my dog's veterinarian was a lesbian, I volunteered for her animal rescue after work, just to have somewhere I didn't feel awkward.

We moved to Cleveland, and I got a federal job in the largest office I had ever worked in. The head of our office, who was also the head of the national headquarters for our division, was an openly gay man. My neighbors were lesbians and not afraid who knew it. Not that everyone was out—I went to a wedding, and a woman my age confessed that her mother was a lesbian, and begged me not to tell a soul, because her mother would lose her job. She was nearly crying with fear that I wouldn't keep her secret. I understood. My husband had told me there was no place for my rainbow hand towels in our new home, and so those had to go. Away from Key West, I still knew what it was like to need to hide.

I got divorced again. I started to write about how much my femininity was an intentional construct, how

I always felt like an impostor. I dated a few women, but I still liked kissing men better. That still wasn't it, but I didn't know what *it* was. I started to realize that my inability to fit in with the straight world was not entirely about having a lesbian mother. As a woman in a group of women, I sometimes felt like I was visiting a foreign country where I was the outsider who used slang slightly incorrectly, or perhaps I was the deaf woman who couldn't hear herself speak so I emphasized the wrong syllables. I was neither fluent nor effortless, and try as I might, I would never be a native speaker. I couldn't say why I felt that I was not quite a real woman. I was a swirl of male and female, and while I did not want to explain it to people, I wanted to be understood so damn badly. Every man I had loved possessed some trait that was not entirely masculine: a lock of hair, a curve of hip, a mincing walk. Sometimes it was in the way they held their hands when they chopped vegetables or in how they cried too much at movies. Regardless, it was always the part that didn't fit with the whole of their masculinity that made me love them.

It wasn't until I found a man who saw my bidrogyny and saw me beautiful not in spite of it, but because of it, that I understood where I fit. He had long hair, I had short. We were the same height, wore the same size clothing and shoes. We were two nonconforming halves that made sense together. I was no longer concerned about how other people defined me.

I HAVE TWO children now, and they don't care that they have more grandmas than their friends do. When my parents come to my children's birthday parties, I introduce them as my parents, not my mom and my aunt, like when I was a kid. My sons know that they can marry a boy or a girl, or no one at all. They understand that how you feel on the inside doesn't always match how your body looks on the outside. They can wear pink or paint their toenails if they want to. They can also play sports and buzz their hair. None of that has to mean anything, unless they want it to. They get to define themselves, and their definitions can change as they grow—they don't have to commit to anything.

WHEN I GREW UP, I didn't know many children with LGBTQ+ parents. I straddled two worlds, and felt like an outsider in both. Now my worlds have come together, and for my kids, there is no separation at all.

CHANGING THE DEFINITION OF GAY

REBECCA GORMAN, age 19

I'M NOT SURE if I can point to a single moment in my childhood and say "Yes, this is *exactly* when I realized my family was different." It is difficult to understand your life experience as uncharacteristic when it is all you have ever known. To me, being raised by a mother and father is impossible to imagine. I have two moms and have felt loved and wanted my entire life. This is my definition of a family.

My parents' identities did not drastically change my experience growing up. I doubt I was even mature enough to understand the concept of sexuality until at least the third grade. Mostly, we did relatively "normal" family things. My moms helped with my homework after school, cooked and ate big meals together, and played with me outside for endless hours. However, being raised by queer mothers has its obvious downfalls, which can be understood by simply flipping through any of the family photo albums from my childhood.

Their understanding of this concept called "fashion" was nonexistent, and hilariously stereotypical. It didn't help that my brother was only two years older than I, and oversized hand-me-downs were a constant in our house. Until I got tired of being called a tomboy, my usual outfit consisted of oversized T-shirts and shorts down to my calves. If they were trying to be stylish that morning, perhaps some lovely clashing pairing of stripes and plaid.

Learning how to dress myself was one of the greatest accomplishments of my life to date. It wasn't very easy making friends while looking like a sack of potatoes who had just rolled out of bed. Explaining the cosmetics I wanted for my birthday or why I wanted to start shaving my legs were somewhat awkward conversations, but puberty isn't exactly comfortable for anyone. It helped that I had an aunt who called herself a "lipstick lesbian" and ran a beauty school. She certainly assisted my fashion needs a smidge.

Our house was briefly in chaos during the two years my mothers simultaneously went through menopause. My brother and I were in an endless battle with them over temperature controls in the house and car. Apparently, menopause and the resulting hot flashes were justifiable excuses to leave the windows open in the middle of a Boston winter. Besides the general confusion with femininity and the extra *spice* that came with so much estrogen, growing up with two moms was relatively normal.

I don't think that lacking a male mentor or a father figure in my life was detrimental to either my childhood development or my relationships with men. The values you learn from your parents are not based on their gender or sexuality. If anything, I would imagine that being raised by two queer women born in the 1960s gave me more exposure to important values such as empathy, acceptance, and resilience. My mothers also demonstrated to my brother and me what a healthy relationship looks like, and the importance of shared responsibilities. In some of my friends' households growing up, their dads worked and fixed things up around the house, while their moms watched the kids and cooked dinner. My house was never like that.

I am thankful to not have been taught to think in such a gendered way. Since my infancy, my parents balanced the responsibilities that come with raising a family—not based on their gender, but on what would be the best for everyone. They both worked, they both cooked. And they expected us to learn things as well and do chores. I knew how to cook, clean, and do laundry way before many of my peers. This came in handy later in life as I sought my independence.

I have thought about—and was asked a surprising amount of times while growing up by curious people—how I think my life may have been different if I had had a father, and I honestly cannot even imagine it. Just because my childhood experience was different from the majority of my peers does not mean that it was inferior in any way. I love my parents, and they have always been enough for me.

However, when I reflect on my experience being raised by queer parents, I cannot help but think of the feeling of embarrassment about my family that I struggled with. I often reflect on where the shame of having two moms originated from. Yes, my family was different, but different is not synonymous to immoral, wrong, or corrupt. I sometimes think it was intrinsically formulated—my own irrational insecurity spurred from the anxiety I have struggled with since I was a child. But I think it was rather people's constant perplexity about the fact that my family was different that caused the humiliation that I began to associate with talking about my moms.

Regardless of whether or not someone intends to be homophobic, to the shy five-year-old being asked if their dad has red hair by the lady at Supercuts, choosing to say "yes" instead of having to explain how their family is different is an obvious choice. As a child, there was nothing I wanted more than to get rid of the messy mop of red ringlets that framed my freckled cheeks. People would see my rusty afro and immediately feel invited to inquire where it came from. I remember hiding in the bottom of the grocery cart, or stuffing my head under my mother's shirt, to avoid the shame-filled attention that followed me everywhere I went.

Questions about genealogy were not the only source of confusion and anxiety that were the result of my parents' sexuality. A lot of times during school, I would be reminded of how different I was. Before every parent-teacher night, I remember teacher after teacher standing up in front of the class letting us all know how "truly excited" they were to meet our moms and dads." Every time I was given a form to bring home for my parents to fill out, I'd have to cross out the line that said "father's signature" and replace it with "mother #2." There was, and *is*, a general expectation about what the "normal" family looks like. Teachers, and classmates, tended to assume that everyone's experiences growing up were the same. We were in the suburbs of Boston, after all—it's hard to imagine a place more focused on achieving what society has defined as the "perfect" American dream. Fences were painted white, not rainbow.

Upon reflection, I wonder how much of my teachers' assumptions about having a homogenous classroom influenced the experiences of bullying or exclusion that I faced from my classmates. To this day, I still vividly recall my childhood struggle to understand the embarrassment I felt and tried to push away. I can replay in my mind the moments of humiliation, and it's hard for me to accept that I was embarrassed by my parents. It seemed that none of my friends were embarrassed of their families, so why should I be? Nevertheless, the fear of being "outed" was a constant in elementary and middle school. Nothing made me cringe more than the simple question, "Do you have two moms?"

Difference is uncomfortable, especially when you are ten years old. Classmates sometimes didn't know how to react to my family, so their way of coping with their discomfort was to ridicule. I often found myself at the center of classmates' jokes or laughter. One day in third grade, the boy to my left turned to me as my classmate got up to speak at our school assembly, and whispered facetiously into my ear, "Did you hear that the new kid has two dads?" The shivers spurred from the laugh that followed still radiate down my spine. He didn't know that I had two moms, otherwise he wouldn't have made the comment. Regardless, the damage was done. *Is this what people say behind my back?* I thought.

I was terrified that my family situation would be exposed to my classmates, and I would be the target of jokes and teasing. I remember a certain day in fifth grade. We were switching classrooms, transitioning from history to math, and were told to wait outside the next class until the teacher was ready for us. The klutz that my ADHD-rushing-self was, I tripped over my own feet and sent my pencil case crashing to the floor. The contents scattered in every direction, and as I scrambled to collect my mess, one of the girls in my class said the last thing I possibly could have wanted to hear: "Don't you have two moms?" If the eyes of all my classmates were not on me before, they most certainly were after that shocking question. It was a question that felt to me like an accusation. The intention was most likely one of curiosity rather than spite, but it felt like a dagger to my heart.

After-school pick-ups always brought anxiety. I tried to run out of there as fast as I possibly could before my peers got a good look at who was in the pick-up line. I dreaded every time one of my friends would ask me who the woman was that picked me up. When I responded "my mom," the next question was always "well, who's the other woman, then?" "That's also my mom." I walked away briskly, leaving them stuck in their bewilderment. Sometimes I was thankful that one of my moms' hair was nearly all grey—hopeful that my classmates would just assume she was my grandmother. Those who were clever enough to figure out my family situation and accept it were the people who I trusted as my friends.

Inviting someone over for an after-school playdate required slightly more consideration than it would for the normal elementary school kid. I would find myself assessing how I thought my potential playmates would react to my family photos on the wall—containing two moms, instead of one. If I judged their character sound, I would bring them home and show them my life. Friendship meant more to me than just enjoying spending time with someone; it meant that I trusted them enough to show them my whole self. I could expose my vulnerabilities to them, and when they responded with love and respect, I cherished them. As I grew up, I collected a widening circle of people that I felt I could trust with my life. I let more people into my life, so more people knew about my family. My teammates and classmates began to know that I was "the girl with two moms," and for the most part, they were okay with that.

Although I still would occasionally find myself doubting whether or not to "out" my family, the amount of embarrassment I felt in regard to my moms had significantly dissipated by the time I entered high school. I think this was partially due to how involved I was with sports—my teammates were quickly exposed to my parents coming to watch me play. They, in many ways, set a respectful norm in which my classmates would interact with me about my family—and many got to know and love my moms. I also think that the increase in social media use helped provide me with a platform on which I could write about and share my family with my peers, while slightly protected by the comfort of a keyboard. Through a single post I could show all of my followers my wonderful family; it alleviated me from being confronted with the oh-so dreaded, "Who are those two women who always pick you up after school?" types of questions.

Although the moment at which I first began to struggle with my own homophobic shame is vague, I can clearly remember the instant I overcame all fear I had previously had with being open about my family. It was a Monday night, six o'clock, November of 2014, and I had just begun the classic post-practice race to finish my homework. I had a research paper due later that week, a muckraking essay about human rights, and had yet to put together so much as an introduction paragraph. I slid three fingers across my mouse pad, bringing up my MacBook's dictionary application. My tenth-grade self, thinking that a definition was the perfect opening line to a serious paper on same-sex marriage, typed the word "*gay*" into the search bar. My glazed eyes read over the results quickly, then stopped midway down the page. I felt my palms begin to sweat and stomach turn, the same familiar feeling I got after hearing someone say, "that's so gay" in the hallway. Praying my vision was deceiving me, I reread the definition: "stupid; foolish: *making students wait for the light is kind of a gay rule.*"

Although I was not surprised to see gay defined that way, I felt disheartened to have society's colloquial and outright hurtful use of the word recognized by one of the most commonly used dictionaries in the world. What I felt in that moment wasn't just disappointment with the definition, but a feeling of illegitimacy; I felt as though the world was defining my family as stupid. Without realizing it at the time, I made a decision as I read that definition: I was done submitting to the voices in my society telling me that I was supposed to be ashamed by my family.

What happened in the next twenty-four hours remains somewhat of a blur. I wrote a letter addressed to Tim Cook, the CEO of Apple, and received a phone call an hour after pressing send. An administrator talked unconvincingly for two minutes, promising that ""maybe they would eventually fix the problem." I wrote ten emails to newspapers across the country asking for their help. By the next day, a Google search of my name resulted in over thirty-four pages of domestic and international news sites. ABC, NBC, and FOX showed up at my doorstep, and the *Ellen DeGeneres Show* appeared on my caller ID.

As I sat on our old red couch staring at FOX News on the screen in front of me, I could not help but become mesmerized by the familiar face reflected back at me. The news reporter's sharp voice broke me from my trance: "Fifteen-year-old Becca Gorman, the daughter of two lesbians, is campaigning to redefine the word *gay*." I perked up as I heard my name, becoming once again entranced by the rather unfamiliar, confident teenager standing up against one of the world's largest companies: Apple. The auburn hair was the same shade as mine, the red couch imprinted with the same stains and memories, and the voice one I recognized as my own, yet something felt different; something had changed in the past forty-eight hours, whether or not my wide-eyed, passionate teenage self was aware of it.

After my efforts, I discovered that Webster's definition of *gay* had been updated earlier that year to include the word *offensive*. The Apple dictionary was later updated to include the same. Upon reflection, I think what mattered the most to me was not that the definition was actually changed. Rather, I wanted the world to know that using a word that people identify with as an insult is degrading. I hoped that by sharing my own story I could communicate the effects of their actions.

Eventually, my fifteen minutes of fame came to an end, and my story drifted to the back burner. But I emerged with a strengthened sense of understanding that I value dearly to this day: my family is something that I should and do feel proud of, and I could not care less if anyone thinks otherwise. What for years brought on feelings of shame now fills me with pride. My two moms are one of my favorite things to talk about. I am incredibly thankful to have such kind, supportive parents, and I want to share that gratitude with the rest of the world.

Six short months following my discovery of the newfound pride I felt towards my family was the momentous day that will go down in history as the day that love won. On June 26, 2015, the Supreme Court of the United States ruled that marriage equality was a constitutional right. I think that day was probably one of the happiest for gay families all across the country. I mean, who could want more than endless rainbow flags and drag marches as far as the eye could see? I spent my "Love Wins" day with my two moms in NYC, marching along in the annual drag parade covered in glitter and rainbow gear headed towards the Stonewall Inn. I can assure you that this was, without a doubt, the gayest thing that I have ever done—and my God, was it fabulous.

In the years following, I continued to kindle my

pride for my family and my involvement in LGBTQ+ family rights and advocacy work. It's not uncommon to see me rocking my rainbow socks on any given day of the week. I love introducing my friends to my parents, and practically show them off and gloat about them as a five-year-old would his new toy at show-and-tell. I guess that is the result of fifteen years of pent-up emotions. There's nothing I wish more than to be able to go back and sit down with my six-year-old self. I would do anything to erase the years of shame and embarrassment that weighed down on me, for what I see now as superfluous reasons.

If I *could* tell anything to my younger self—besides start watching fashion shows ASAP—it would be that if you feel like you have to hide any part of yourself for another person, they probably aren't worth your time, anyway. Some of my closest friends to this day are the ones I felt comfortable enough to bring home for after-school playdates; or the friends who would laugh along with me and my moms carpooling to softball practice. Hiding a beautifully unique part of your identity serves no one. After all, they don't say we were raised by unicorns for nothing.

BEAUTY AND THE BUTCH

AN INTERVIEW WITH JOE VALENTINE, age 38

AS THE EDITOR of this anthology, I had the privilege of hearing from many different people, from all walks of life. It was truly an enlightening experience and gave me a greater sense of empathy. One of the gentlemen I had the pleasure to speak with was ex-major league baseball pitcher, Joe Valentine. Together, we decided to do his chapter more like an interview, so I sat down with him and we just chatted. Here is the result—it's a very enjoyable story and a true depiction of LGBTQ+ family life.

Frank Lowe: I guess the most obvious question is, tell me about your family. You grew up with two moms?

Joe Valentine: Well, so I was born into my gay parents, my lesbian parents, at birth.

FL: One of them carried you?

JV: One of them did carry me, yes. That is my biological mother, Deborah. My non-biological mother is Doreen. They met in high school, then moved to Las Vegas—what every young lesbian couple in the 70s apparently did. I am their only child.

FL: What year was this?

JV: Yeah, 1979. I was born on Christmas Eve. Spent a few years out there, then they moved back home because the climate changed. The 80s were getting a little too crazy in Vegas.

FL: Did they use a sperm donor or was it a friend? How did they conceive?

JV: Well . . . let's just say it was the 1970s in Las Vegas.

FL: Okay, gotcha. Wow! My follow-up question would then be, have you connected with your biological father at all?

JV: No, I have not and have never really desired to. But I was given the story in essence. It is what it is, you know?

FL: How young were you when they told you that . . . how it all came about?

JV: According to them, I was always pretty in-tune with what was going on, but I started asking questions around four or five. Not super in-depth questions, but people would ask my moms in front of me, "Where's the daddy?" They explained it to me. I never really gave it much thought.

FL: Sure, because you would see other people, or your peers with "traditional families."

JV: Exactly. I definitely was a unicorn. I

definitely was sticking out like a sore thumb myself, but being in New York, it wasn't really a social issue, it was pretty much accepted even in the early 80s.

FL: Did you live in Manhattan?

JV: No, we were actually in the suburbs of Long Island, in a town called North Babylon. We initially lived a few years with Doreen's parents. They had an apartment above their house so we stayed with them. My parents opened up a hair salon, because that's what one of my moms did for a trade. Then we wound up buying a house a few years later. It was just me, my parents, and my grandparents— Grandpa Joe and Grandma Evelyn. They were my immediate family that were very close to me.

A funny thing to mention is that my mother, Doreen, has two siblings, and both are gay. My one grandmother who I wound up living with—who is my rock to this day—had three kids, all gay.

FL: All three gay! Now when you say gay, were they all lesbian, gay, or . . . ?

JV: Well, yeah. I'd say gay—a younger brother, and the youngest is her sister.

FL: So two lesbians and a gay man. For those who argue that there's nothing to genetics, then there you go right there, that's pretty much proof-positive. What about your other mom, Deborah's side of the family?

JV: They are very prim and proper, and didn't speak much about the family dynamic.

FL: Well, I can at least imagine Thanksgivings must be very interesting.

JV: Let's just try not to fight, you know?

FL: Do I ever! Are your moms similar to each other or more opposites?

JV: My moms are literally "Beauty and the Butch." Deborah—Deb—is the beauty queen. She was the hair stylist, she always wore high-fashion clothes, and she loved that industry. I guess she's what you'd call a "lipstick lesbian."

Doreen, on the other hand, was a hard-working, blue collar worker. She was the one who would play and get dirty with me. We practiced a lot of baseball together.

FL: I would assume that their dichotomy worked really well as far as parenting is concerned. Give me a quick background about your career and how you got into sports, like what kind of path took you in that direction?

JV: I took the normal path that I think every other kid out there does, really. My parents put me in baseball and soccer and whatever I asked for, and things I didn't even ask for—including dance.

FL: Dance? Tell me more.

JV: I took ballet, I took tap, I took jazz, whatever it was, but I also played a lot of the sports at the same time. Eventually, when I got to be about twelve or thirteen, I was like, okay, putting on the tights and doing all the stuff was getting to me. It was taking away from my passion that was growing into sports.

FL: So at some point, your passion for sports overcame your passion for dancing?

JV: Yeah, my main three staples were dance, soccer, and baseball. And at maybe thirteen or fourteen is when dance started to take a back seat. Then at fifteen, I completely stopped dancing altogether.

FL: Were you getting stigmatized?

JV: Oh, yeah, absolutely. But I quit mainly because soccer and baseball were taking over—they just consumed me. At fifteen, I realized, "Okay, I'm a little bit better than most at sports." I was a very modest kid, but you kind of . . . you just saw what was happening, so I focused on sports.

FL: So then how did that narrow down into baseball?

JV: Living in New York, soccer and baseball are two different seasons—I never had to choose. Baseball was in the spring, soccer was in the fall. Soccer I loved, but I didn't love it as much as baseball, and something was pulling me toward baseball, so I went with it. By the time my senior year arrived, it was strictly just baseball.

FL: Okay, and then I'm going to assume from there you got baseball scholarships to college, is that how it works?

JV: Yeah, so I got a few offers, nothing crazy, and decided on a local college here in Long Island, Dowling College. It was only about fifteen minutes from the house.

I only went there for half a semester—I was not happy. I was feeling *not* ready for college. I was like, if I'm gonna do this, I'm gonna *do this*. I felt like I was living too close to my family. My parents would come pick up my laundry and bring me trays of lasagna. It was too much.

If I was ready, I was ready to go away. I wanted to play baseball, I wanted the full college experience. So I withdrew from Dowling in December. I just stopped going. Then I went back to college the following fall, to a junior college to play baseball in Brewton, Alabama.

FL: Oh, man. That's a switch!

JV: Yeah, yeah. It was a total culture shock. But I was actually at the junior college for a year and then got drafted into pro baseball.

FL: And what was the first team? Did you change teams throughout your career?

JV: I did. I changed quite a bit, actually. There were a few teams that I played on, but I initially got drafted by the Chicago White Sox. I spent a few years there in the minor leagues, then got traded—actually twice within twelve months—to the Oakland A's, and then from there to the big leagues with the Cincinnati Reds.

FL: Did you face any discrimination about having two moms, or did you keep it a secret?

JV: Well, for a while I kept it secret. I wanted to have somewhat of a cemented feeling about myself being in the big leagues. I didn't break out and tell my story until 2005, and Cincinnati was still very red at that time.

FL: Understandable.

JV: I had to make sure that I was in an okay place to be able to do it, and I spoke with a couple of PR people about it, and it just so happened to come up when I was being interviewed with my local paper here in New York, and he said, "Can I ask for your parents' names?" And I told him. Without even thinking, the interviewer goes, "Wait, what?"

FL: I doubt he was expecting that answer!

JV: Jeff Pearlman is his name. I'll never forget his name. And he goes, "Wait, what?" I go, "Deb and Doreen." I spelled out, "D-O-R-E-E-N." And he said, "Are you telling me you have two moms?" I go, "Yeah, why?" He says, "Don't you know this is a big fuckin' deal?" I go, "Off the record, this is *my* life, right?"

FL: Exactly.

JV: I said, "It's not really a big deal, it is what it is." He replied, "We have to put this out. You're a professional athlete that's grown up with two moms." I said, "Not only did I grow up with two moms, but they're also not what I call a conversion family. Like Mom and Dad have kids and all of a sudden one of them realizes, 'hey, this is not for me.'"

FL: Which is a very common thing that occurs, unfortunately.

JV: But yeah, so then I talked to my parents and

talked to the people that were around me, the loved ones, and they said, "How do you feel about it?" I said, "I don't really feel any way about it because it's so natural for me to talk about it. So . . . "

You know you're gonna get some backlash. Listen, if I can't deal with it, I can't deal with it. I'll be all right. Then the story broke, and that's when backlash ensued. But a lot more positives than negatives—the positives outweighed them exponentially. I have printed out emails that I received from kids, parents, aunts, uncles, *whoever*, that thanked me for coming forward.

FL: Yeah. Definitely. That's so awesome you could do that. My next question would be, prior to that moment, what would you tell people?

JV: You know, for a long, long time, my cover-up, even with my best friends and people I was close to, was, "This is my mother, and this is my aunt." You know, my friends came over, and they either got it, or didn't get it. Like, "Where's your aunt?"

FL: There was no one who ever came over and tried to call you out or something like that? That never happened?

JV: It happened a few times in high school. And at that point, I'd go, "Yeah, two moms. What are *you* gonna do about it? Step outside, if you have a problem with it."

Because one, I was bigger and stronger than most, and two, I'd say, "Who've you been talking to?" I would say something athletically to make 'em feel inferior, or whatever.

FL: So you used words. Words were your weapons.

JV: Yeah, then it would really hush them up really quickly. And the one line that I always used, and it was only once I was older, to be able to verbalize and feel who I was, was, "I got a lot of things in my life that are gonna be bigger than you and this moment, so I'm not gonna ruin it for this."

FL: That's excellent, that you had that instilled in you.

JV: I'd kinda leave it at that and walk away.

My parents always said, "In that moment, you always have bigger and better things that are going to be ahead of you, so don't waste it on that one time that you lose your temper." Doreen, who is the butch one, would secretly add, "Rip his fucking head off." And my mother Deborah, would be like, "Just don't ruin your cheekbones." You know, this was a long time ago. Like, don't get any facial scars.

FL: Right, right. Avoid fighting if you can, *but if you must*, don't hurt your pretty face. I love that, that's great.

From your observation, what would you say is the most significant difference about having both gay parents versus straight ones?

JV: I don't know. I had my eyebrows tweezed, at like twelve. I knew how to verbally attack someone. I grew up in a hair salon, it was a gay community, it was gay men, women, whatever. But I think the biggest benefit was seeing that it didn't matter. It didn't matter what color, what creed, what sexual orientation, big, small, it didn't matter.

FL: So you're saying the big difference is that there was no difference. It was just intrinsic to you, almost engraved in you, from birth essentially.

JV: Yeah.

FL: Your experience was no different than any others, in your eyes.

JV: No, it wasn't, and I swear that it helped me become a better person, because I didn't have any bigoted comments being flung around my house. It wasn't made a big deal. And what I saw was people just loving each other for who they were, at an early age. I knew we were different, but it didn't matter, it just didn't matter.

FL: Was there ever a time or moment that your peers were talking negatively about LGBTQ+ people, and it made you feel uncomfortable or ashamed? And then, how did you handle that, if so? Not necessarily talking about your moms specifically, but just in general. You know, you hear the word *faggot*, or *dyke*, or something like that.

JV: The actual words never really affected me. It was the connotation, it was the story behind it. During my childhood, if another kid said, "Don't be a fag," it didn't carry the weight that it does now, because I was a kid. But *now* it does. Some of those words are just . . . to me, it breaks my spirit.

silence

But there were very few times that I ever had to say something. There's only a couple moments in my career that I felt compelled to speak up.

FL: Okay, so this is now in your adult life, is what you're saying. Not—

JV: I never felt compelled to then go after a fellow friend or companion in school, because one, I felt like I was more mature than everybody else. And I also said, "They don't know what the hell they're saying, so why even waste my breath?"

FL: Right. They're ignorant, essentially.

JV: Yeah, they're ignorant.

And one time when I did feel the need, it was actually the same day that I was speaking to the reporter and told him my parents' names. I'm talking about two hours prior to this call.

We were in the bullpen. Typically, there were three things we didn't talk about in the bullpen: religion, politics, or sexual orientation. Like those were just three things in pro sports you really didn't talk about.

FL: Those are excellent parameters if people actually followed them.

JV: Somehow we got into the topic of gay parents. A teammate, who I will leave unnamed, said to all, "Well, anybody raised by gay or lesbian parents has to become fucked up."

And so I said . . . I sat there for about five seconds and I kind of just looked at him. I said, "Hey man, what do you think of me?" He goes "What do you mean, what do I think of you? I think you're a great guy, a little too pretty for my liking." I go, "Yeah!" I said this didn't happen by mistake and I've always said that. There's a lot of effort that goes into how I look and that's because of my parents—I was a pretty boy.

Then he goes, "Well, what are you saying?" I go, "Dude, I was raised by lesbians." He's like, "Get the fuck outta here, there's no way! You gotta be bullshitting."

So, I didn't say anything and two minutes later he goes, "Wait, are you serious?" I replied, "Yeah, serious as a heart attack."

I go, "How do you feel about it now?" And he said, "Well, I guess I just put my foot in my mouth."

I kept on with, "I'm not trying to put your foot in your mouth, but don't judge a book by its cover. By your thinking, I was going to be fucked up. I'm the most normal dude you know. You know, right here and now."

And that was it, there was no animosity, there was no nothing.

FL: I'm sure he was shocked and embarrassed.

JV: It was a pretty enlightening moment for him. He came up to me about twenty minutes later and said, "Dude, never think of that situation ever again."

FL: Yep. He felt—

JV: He was disappointed in himself. And then literally two hours later, at the end of the game, is when I did the interview explaining I have two moms.

FL: Do you think that incident in the bullpen inspired you to do the interview?

JV: It was a gate opening. Yeah, I think that was definitely the gate opening.

When the story actually broke, I had some people who I felt would distance themselves from me. Baseball is a very southern sport. I'm a New Yorker. Raised by lesbians. The friends I was making there were few and far between.

FL: Tell me a little bit about your home life now. You have a wife and two daughters, correct?

JV: That's correct, she's my second wife. My *first* wife was my high school sweetheart. We were together for thirteen years, married just under five. We just grew apart. We weren't the same people that we fell in love with in high school.

FL: That's common.

JV: Yeah. Everything kinda got into it, and we ended up splitting up and going separate ways. I met my current wife, Lauren, on Match.com.

FL: Have there ever been any issues with those you dated, etc. or their family members, in regards to you having two moms?

JV: My first wife—yeah, she was understanding. Her parents were completely tolerant. And fortunately my current wife and her family are completely accepting. They're like, "You're a grown man. They're your grown parents. No big deal."

But . . . when I went down to Alabama, I briefly

split with my high school sweetheart, my first wife. Of course, I fell in love with a southern blonde bombshell, and was with her for three months, during which I was perceived like the antichrist. It was in the Deep South, and I'm such a New Yorker.

FL: It was all very foreign to you and you weren't comfortable with it. So did you ever bring up your family with them?

JV: Oh, yeah, my parents came down. They met her and her family. We had to introduce them to her parents as my staple go-to—my mom and my aunt.

Then after like a month of that, I think I had a beer or two or otherwise. Somebody from her family said to me, "Your mother and her sister look nothing alike." I go, "That's because they're not sisters. They're lovers. Those are my parents."

And I was basically asked to leave the house that night. Yeah. My girlfriend at the time was saying, "You can't leave, I love you. I want to get married. I *love* you."

So that began the deterioration of the relationship, because they were Southern Baptist, and were probably the biggest bigots I've ever met in my life. I had a tattoo as well, which apparently was the mark of the devil.

FL: Oh, I'm sure. I'm sure. I can only imagine what you endured.

JV: Here's the kicker: in the midst of all this turmoil, her mother got a boob job. And then proclaimed things to her daughter/my girlfriend like, "I think he's the devil, or the spirit of the devil." Because she'd say like, he's trying to take my daughter's virginity.

FL: Oh my God!

JV: So, I was already calling her "Mom," because that's what she wanted. "Mom," I said. "Why'd you get the boobs?" And she looked at me. And she's like, "What do you mean?" I go, "Who are you trying to impress? God didn't give you those, right?" And she said, "God knows that I have self-esteem issues." So I replied "And God knows I love my friends so much that I got a tattoo to remember them, so it helps me, too."

FL: Good for you. Amen.

JV: My message to her mom was clear: if I'm going to hell, you're going to hell. Then I looked at my girlfriend, and decided, "I don't think this is going to work out."

However, I kept *trying* to make it work. We hung in there for a few more months, but six months later, it was over. I told her, "You need to be around more open-minded people in your life to live a full one."

FL: I love that you said that. That's great.

JV: For me, to be honest, it was kind of fun. It was the first time that I really didn't give a shit about somebody's feelings, because she and her family clearly didn't give a shit about mine.

FL: No, no. They were using "the church" and

God to suit their means. Like whatever their needs of the day were.

JV: Yeah, you're right. Like I was actually trying to take her daughter's virginity and spawn the devil's devil. I quickly got out of there, and it was a mother waste of time, but it felt vindicating. I mean, for like an eighteen-year-old's tattoo that was probably three inches in diameter—to tell me I'm going to hell [for that], yet you can show 48DDs, that's so hypocritical. If God wanted you to have big tits, you'd have big tits.

FL: Anything else come to mind in regards to growing up or your moms?

JV: I had a very close relationship with one of my best friends, and we'd go down to Gatlinburg, Tennessee for like two weeks at a time. There were many trips to Dollywood. I had what I consider a very normal childhood, which surprises people. People will say, "You have?" And I'm like, "Yeah. I went on vacation with other families." My parents weren't aliens.

FL: See, that's what so funny about this whole thing. People get so shocked by the normalcy of gay parents and what not.

JV: Yeah. It's perfectly normal. For me, it most certainly was normal.

FL: Well, sure.

JV: My parents would go to soccer tournaments, and they'd be getting drunk with the other parents. And then, of course, sleep together while on a sleep-away tournament, you know. My parents did all those things.

FL: Well, Joe, thank you so much for talking to me. It further proves my theory that gay families are no different than straight families. It makes me happy to hear you had such a wonderful childhood and support system. Your moms sound incredible!

JV: Absolutely. If there's one thing I want to stress, it's that my moms were awesome and always did whatever they needed to do to make sure I was happy. If that's not amazing parenting, I don't know what is.

RESOURCES

BOOKS

The Kid: What Happened After My Boyfriend and I Decided to Go Get Pregnant - Dan Savage (Penguin Books, 2000)

Out of the Ordinary: Essays on Growing Up with Gay, Lesbian, and Transgender Parents – Noelle Howey and Ellen Samuels (Stonewall Inn Editions, 2000)

Dress Codes: Of Three Girlhoods – My Mother's, My Father's, and Mine – Noelle Howey (Virago Press Ltd, 2003)

How It Feels to Have a Gay or Lesbian Parent – Judith E. Snow, MA (Routledge, 2004)

Families Like Mine: Children of Gay Parents Tell it Like it Is – Abigail Garner (Harper Perennial, 2005)

Confessions of the Other Mother - Harlyn Aizley (Beacon Press, 2006)

Let's Get this Straight: The Ultimate Handbook for Youth with LGBTQ Parents – Tina Fakhrid-Deen (Seal Press, 2010)

Does This Baby Make Me Look Straight?: Confessions of a Gay Dad - Dan Bucatinsky (Touchstone, 2012)

Confessions of a Fairy's Daughter: Growing Up with a Gay Dad – Alison Wearing (Knopf Canada, 2013)

Fairyland: A Memoir of My Father – Alysia Abbot (W. W. Norton & Company, 2013)

Family Pride: What LGBT Families Should Know about Navigating Home, School, and Safety in Their Neighborhoods (Queer Ideas/Queer Action) – Michael Shelton (Beacon Press, 2013)

My Two Moms: Lessons of Love, Strength, and What Makes a Family – Zach Wahls (Avery, 2013)

Mom, I'm Gay – Susan Cottrell (Westminster John Knox Press, 2016)

Queerspawn in Love: A Memoir – Kellen Anne Kaiser (She Writes Press, 2016)

A Bigger Table– John Pavlovitz (Westminster John Knox Press, 2017)

Changing our Mind – David P. Gushee (Read the Spirit Books, 2017)

The Ultimate Guide for Gay Dads: Everything You Need to Know About LGBTQ Parenting But Are (Mostly) Afraid to Ask - Eric Rosswood (Mango, 2017)

Girlish: Growing Up in a Lesbian Home - Lara Lillibridge (Skyhorse Publishing, 2018)

WEBSITES

Advocate
    https://www.advocate.com
COLAGE: People with a Lesbian, Gay, Bisexual, Trans-
    gender, or Queer Parent
    https://www.colage.org/
Eliel Cruz & The Anti-Violence Project
    http://elielcruz.com/
Faith in America
    http://www.faithinamerica.org/
Family Equality Council
    https://www.familyequality.org/
Freed Hearts
    https://www.freedhearts.org/
Gays with Kids
    https://www.gayswithkids.com/
HuffPost
    https://www.huffingtonpost.com/section/queer-voices
Human Rights Campaign
    https://www.hrc.org/
It Gets Better Project
    https://itgetsbetter.org
The Next Family
    http://thenextfamily.com/
One Million Kids for Equality
    https://onemillionkids.org/
OUT
    https://www.out.com
Queer Christian Fellowship
    https://www.qchristian.org/

Rainbow Letters Project
    http://www.therainbowletters.com/
The Reformation Project
    https://www.reformationproject.org/
Trans Youth Equality Foundation
    http://www.transyouthequality.org
The Trevor Project
    https://www.thetrevorproject.org/

DOCUMENTARIES, MOVIES, AND VIDEOS

Our House – PBS (2000)
Southern Comfort – Kate Davis (2001)
Myth of Father – Paul Hill (2003)
In My Shoes – COLAGE (2005)
From This Day Forward – Sharon Shattuck (2015)
Gayby Baby – Maya Newell (2015)

ABOUT THE AUTHOR

 FRANK LOWE is a gay, divorced, forty-one-year-old dad. He is best known for his acerbic handle on Twitter (@GayAtHomeDad), and has worked for publications such as *The Advocate*, HuffPost, and Gays with Kids. His goal was to bring comedic attention to the now not-so-unique world of gay parenting. As a result, he has been interviewed by CNN, CBS, *OUT*, Ozy, HuffPost, and *The Today Show*, to name a few. His life mission is to remove the word "gay" from the phrase "gay parenting." He currently lives in Northwestern Connecticut with his eight-year-old son.